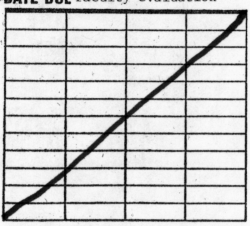

Changing Practices
in Faculty Evaluation

*A Critical Assessment
and Recommendations
for Improvement*

Peter Seldin

Changing Practices
in Faculty Evaluation

Jossey-Bass Publishers

San Francisco • Washington • London • 1984

CHANGING PRACTICES IN FACULTY EVALUATION
A Critical Assessment and Recommendations for Improvement
by Peter Seldin

Copyright © 1984 by: Jossey-Bass Inc., Publishers
433 California Street
San Francisco, California 94104
&
Jossey-Bass Limited
28 Banner Street
London EC1Y 8QE

Library of Congress Cataloging in Publication Data

Seldin, Peter.
   Changing practices in faculty evaluation.

   Bibliography: p. 183
   Includes index.
   1. College teachers—Rating of—United States.
2. Universities and colleges—United States—Faculty.
   I. Title.
LB2333.S437   1984   378'.12   83-49268
ISBN 0-87589-601-4

Manufactured in the United States of America

The paper in this book meets the guidelines for
permanence and durability of the Committee on
Production Guidelines for Book Longevity of the
Council on Library Resources.

JACKET DESIGN BY WILLI BAUM

FIRST EDITION

Code 8410

*The Jossey-Bass
Higher Education Series*

To my parents, Rose and Joseph Seldin, whose strong support was as firm as ever; and to my family — my wife, Pat, and our children Marc, Amy, and Nancy — for their cheerful encouragement and willingness to give up much of our time together during the writing of this book.

Preface

In their rush to make judgments on tenure, promotion, and retention — accelerated in recent years due to increased costs, shortage of funds, dropping enrollments, and incipient competition from large corporations entering higher education — many colleges and universities are embracing seriously flawed faculty evaluation programs. Inadequate, biased, or worse, such programs yield a harvest of faculty resistance and, not infrequently, court challenges that reverse improper administrative decisions.

Intended for administrators and faculty, the essential partners in the development of successful evaluation programs, this book distills the literature and even more, my own personal experience for more than a decade in the improvement of faculty evaluation programs. It reveals changes and emerging trends from the third nationwide study I have conducted of policies and practices in assessing faculty performance. This book will provide both administrators and faculty with an opportunity to compare current evaluation practices and to learn from others' experience how to improve their own. To be consistent with the 1978 and 1973 investigations, the current study focuses on the liberal arts college. Administrators and faculty of professional colleges will discover that the problems and solutions in establishing evaluation programs are readily transferable. They will find many applications in the study to professional colleges.

Chapter One examines the root causes of today's crisis in higher education, describes survival strategies used by colleges and universities, and relates the search for solvency to major changes in assessing faculty performance.

Chapter Two scrutinizes the proliferation of court challenges to administrative decisions on promotion, tenure, retention, the legal right of "discovery" versus the academic tradition
of confidentiality, the ripple effect of landmark legal decisions,
and the extension of civil rights legislation to faculty evaluation
programs.

Chapter Three defines my 1983 study of policies and practices of 616 public and private liberal arts colleges in evaluating
teaching, research, and service for faculty promotion, tenure, and
retention decisions; compares the 1983 study with the 1978 and
1973 studies; and contains 31 tables and graphs on key changes
and trends.

Chapter Four consists of remarks by seven commentators,
each prominent in faculty evaluation, who offer diverse and critical observations on the 1983 study and its implications for higher
education; and my reflections on key issues raised by the commentators.

Chapter Five is based on my experience in assisting
numerous colleges and universities to develop faculty evaluation
programs. It describes the step-by-step construction of successful
programs, and covers student-, colleague-, and self-evaluation, as
well as research and publication, and institutional and community service. It contains tested and proved appraisal forms.

Earlier books on faculty evaluation have taken a broad,
how-to approach and been geared primarily to institutions that
are just setting up their faculty evaluation programs. This book
has a different thrust. It studies the transformation of faculty evaluation systems over the past decade; it points out implications for
the future; it provides institutions with a chance to compare practices; it spells out the important legal considerations that impact
today on evaluation systems; and it specifies the key elements of
existing systems that must be improved in order to strengthen the
overall system.

Administrators and faculty members both in private and
public colleges and universities will be able to take new bearings
from the changes and trends noted in the following pages. The
language is straightforward and nontechnical.

I am grateful to Pace University for providing the scholarly research grant for the national study summarized in this book. Special thanks to deans T. H. Bonaparte, John McCall, and Walter Joyce and department chairman Robert Dennehy for their consistent encouragement and assistance throughout this project.

Croton-on-Hudson, New York   Peter Seldin
Februrary 1984

Contents

Contents

Tables, Figures, and Exhibits

Tables

Figures

Exhibits

The Author

Peter Seldin is professor of management at Pace University, Pleasantville, New York. He received his B.A. degree (1963) from Hobart College in psychology, his M.B.A. degree (1966) from Long Island University in management, and his Ph.D. degree (1974) from Fordham University in education. His postdoctoral work in faculty evaluation and development was at the University of London (1976).

Seldin has served on the editorial board of the quarterly newspaper *Faculty Development and Evaluation in Higher Education*, on the core committee of the Professional and Organizational Development Network, and on the program advisory committee for the International Conference on Improving University Teaching.

His books include *How Colleges Evaluate Professors* (1975), *Teaching Professors to Teach* (1977), and *Successful Faculty Evaluation Programs* (1980). He has contributed numerous articles on faculty evaluation and development to such publications as the *New York Times* and *Change Magazine*.

Seldin has designed and conducted seminars for faculty and administrators in colleges and universities throughout the United States and in Japan, England, Egypt, Germany, and Switzerland. He is a frequent speaker at national and international conferences.

Changing Practices
in Faculty Evaluation

*A Critical Assessment
and Recommendations
for Improvement*

Chapter 1

Fiscal Crisis in Higher Education:
The Search for Solvency and Consequences for Faculty

Faced by an economic squeeze unprecedented in recent years for its severity and duration, the nation's colleges and universities are struggling to cope with reduced budgets, hunting for new money sources, and casting a gimlet eye on which faculty to promote and which courses to teach. The purpose of this chapter is to examine the origins and consequences of the fiscal crunch and to observe how administrators and faculty are reacting to their predicament.

Impact on Public Institutions

If a single statistic can dramatize the economic problems, it is the annual state appropriation for higher education. For the academic year 1982–83, the state appropriation was only 6 percent more than for the preceding year. This was the smallest increase in more than twenty years. For over two decades, the annual increase in appropriation averaged nearly 20 percent. But the economic recession cut deeply into the states' sales and income taxes, and the states shared their hard times with institutions of higher learning. In fact, after adjustment for inflation, the 6 percent increase in state appropriation actually represents, in fixed dollars, a decrease in support for about half the states. Put another

1

way, since the Department of Labor's consumer price index rose 17.4 percent during the two years ending June 30, 1982, the states' two-year appropriation increase of 16 percent represented to colleges and universities a 1 percent loss in purchasing power.

A few more facts and figures paint the picture in even more somber hues. Only twice in the last two decades, in 1962–63 and 1976–77, has the yearly growth in state funding dipped as low as 9 percent. By comparison, during the boom years in the late 1960s, the yearly growth in state largesse to higher education twice reached 25 percent, in 1965–66 and 1967–68.

Facing overwhelming economic problems, many presidents of public colleges and universities have given grim voice to the national predicament of higher education. The *Chronicle of Higher Education* recently queried a number of presidents of colleges and universities on the financial condition of their institutions. Two thirds of the public universities and almost half of the four-year colleges reported falling behind financially. Only 17 percent of the public universities and 26 percent of the four-year colleges were able to report a gain (Magarrell, 1982a).

In a worst-case instance, institutions of higher education in Oregon face the most stringent financial problems in the nation, at least so far as state support is concerned. The state appropriation actually dropped by 4 percent for public colleges and universities in 1982–83 from the preceding year. The predictable result was an institutional scramble to cut expenses by a simultaneous freeze on purchasing, hiring, and salaries, the abolition of programs, and the firing of employees.

Impact on Private Institutions

Although private colleges and universities do not depend on the financial lifeline of state support, by no means have they been immune to the economic recession. Many educators and demographers freely predict that as many as 300 colleges will be forced to close by the mid-1990s for lack of students. They predict the greatest demise among private liberal arts institutions. Facing the specter of going out of business, colleges and universities are embracing cost-cutting methods and cultivating new income sources in a frantic race to remain solvent.

Today, colleges and universities are more businesslike, cost controls are far superior to what they were even five years ago, and careful tracking of expenditures, cost-benefit analyses, and line-by-line budget examinations are the norm. College presidents are sought who have exemplary records in management and efficiency. Typically, recent advertisements for presidents in the *New York Times* call for "extensive management experience" or "prior involvement with modern management techniques and budgetary administration."

In recent years, private institutions struggling to balance their budgets have demanded more tuition dollars. Annual tuition increases of 10 percent or more are not unusual. The price tag for tuition, room, and board passed $10,000 per year at many colleges and reached $14,000 at some of the most prestigious institutions.

The Reagan administration, in an effort to cut federal spending, gave top priority to cutting student assistance programs. The annual bill to the federal government for subsidizing the guaranteed student loan program was in the neighborhood of $3 billion. This tidy sum began to shrink with the imposition of a "needs test" that made any student ineligible whose family had an adjusted gross annual income of over $30,000. But cutting the student aid program hit the private colleges particularly hard, since many students counted on government assistance to help cover the high cost of staying in school. This high cost also placed private colleges and universities out of reach for many families with college-bound children. High school guidance counselors reported a growing number of families seriously considering public rather than private institutions. In the fall of 1982, private colleges across the country reported that an unusually large number of enrolled freshmen failed to matriculate because of anxiety over their ability to pay. At Middlebury College (Vermont), for example, out of a class of 500 enrolled freshmen, the number forfeiting deposits increased from 35 to 61.

Other Results of Tight Funds

Private and public colleges have always engaged in parlor-room talk about working together for the common good of higher education. The polite dialogue continues, but evidence of tense competition between the two types of institutions is mounting. What was once a friendly rivalry for program quality is turning into a free-for-all for students and funds. What was once an exchange of pleasantries in the jockeying for position at budget time is turning more frequently into acerbic warfare.

Private colleges, trying to offset tuition increases, are requesting state legislatures to provide more student aid money. Public colleges, trying to maintain quality programs and staff, are going after more private money from corporations, foundations, and alumni.

The scramble for funds produces a doleful picture. In North Carolina, for instance, with state institutions running on austerity programs, bills were introduced in the state legislature to give students in private colleges more financial aid. In Connecticut, a compromise permitted Central Connecticut State University to offer a new graduate business program but required students to take one quarter of the program at the nearby University of Hartford, a private institution. The University of California at Los Angeles, whose private fund raising in 1981–82 was exceeded only by that of Harvard, Yale, and Stanford universities, began toying with a five-year campaign to raise between $150 million and $250 million.

The money crunch has also meant swollen classes for professors. As a worst-case example, the University of Florida in the last twelve years has gained 6,000 students while decreasing its faculty by 100. The classic money-saving device employed by many institutions is foot dragging when it comes to hiring professors to replace those who have resigned or retired.

In addition to swollen classes, the money crunch also affects what is taught in the classes. Since course material is increasingly dictated by the contemporary job market for students, some departments in colleges and universities blossomed with breathtaking speed as other departments withered. For example, Columbia University has a reputation as a center for liberal arts, but computer science is its fastest growing discipline. At Miami University, as one third of the students enrolled in the school of business, the administration placed a lid on the number to prevent their dominating the institution.

It was not only business and computer science that brought changes. The pattern was repeated in accounting, engineering, and nursing. One result was a shortage of professors equipped to teach the popular new courses. But higher salaries became the magnet to attract them. One survey discovered that the average salary for new assistant professors in business, computer science, and engineering was as much as $5,800 higher than for those in foreign languages, history, and English. But the higher salaries paid to qualified professors to teach the new courses collided head on with overall budgetary limitations.

The response at Portland State University, which was typical, was to eliminate nineteen faculty positions, close several research institutions, drop the journalism program, and combine three colleges under one dean. Similarly, the University of Oregon dropped more than seventy faculty and staff positions and closed its Institute for Social Service and its School of Community Service and Public Affairs.

In Michigan, in anticipation of a decade of declining enrollment and shrinking finances, the state legislature demanded a re-examination of the state college system. The legislature voted early in 1983 to establish a panel to study the network of fifteen public universities and twenty-nine community colleges. Some educators feared that the panel was only the first step leading to the closing of several colleges. This fear was given credence by the opinion openly expressed by several lawmakers that fiscal health might require the closing of six of the most recently acquired state colleges. In Michigan's automobile-based economy, higher education took the brunt of cuts in the state budget to the tune of $50 million in 1981 and 1982. Major programs were dropped even at the state's Big Three, the University of Michigan, Michigan State University, and Wayne State University.

The University of Washington announced that it would eliminate twenty-four degree programs and reduce enrollment by nearly 5,000 over the next three years. Degree-program victims included urban planning, nutrition, art education, textiles, children's drama, music education, and dance.

In a startling and desperate move, Westminster College (Utah) announced it was going out of business on June 30, 1983, and would reopen the next morning as Westminster College of Salt Lake City, a new institution with a new charter. All faculty and staff contracts, including those of tenured professors, would automatically be terminated. The college would selectively rehire only those professors and staff who fit into the new structure.

In an equally unusual move, the trustees of Bennington College (Vermont) announced the leasing of the campus to a partnership of wealthy alumni. The partnership would pay $8 million to lease the campus for ninety-nine years. The college would use that money to pay off its debts, enrich its endowment, and repay the partners in small annual installments as rent for use of the campus. The plan paid off for everyone except the I.R.S. The partners enjoyed tax deductions for depreciation of the college property, and Bennington College received the equivalent of an $8 million interest-free loan.

The Enrollment Crunch

As if today's fiscal problems were not enough, campuses around the country are haunted by the knowledge that, for the next fifteen years, the number of college applicants will be appreciably smaller. The postwar "baby-boom" generation has already passed through the nation's colleges and universities, and what remains for the immediate future is the diminished "birth-dearth" generation. From now to the mid-1990s, according to most demographic studies, the number of eighteen-year-olds will drop 26 percent. Since this figure is based on head counts of children already born, it is hard data, not subject to the usual vagaries of a forecast. The sharp drop occurs between 1979 (the peak year) and 1994 (the trough) as the eighteen-year-old population falls from 4.3 million to 3.2 million. No wonder these are anxious years for institutions of higher education.

The problem is expected to be less serious for institutions such as Harvard, Yale, Princeton, and Stanford, because they will continue to attract first-rate students. But for the country's less prestigious colleges and universities, the problem looms as critical. Since colleges and universities ordinarily draw their students from their own states or regional areas, it is expected that the enrollment decline will not be evenly distributed. Such states as New York, Massachusetts, and Connecticut have projected declines of over 40 percent, while Pennsylvania, Maryland, Michigan, and Illinois expect losses of 34 to 40 percent.

Whatever else will happen, intense competition for students among colleges and universities can be predicted with certainty. David Breneman (1983), a senior fellow at the Brookings Institution, suggests that two groups of colleges and universities are particularly at risk, the nonselective private liberal arts colleges and the public state colleges and universities. If so, the problem for the private liberal arts colleges in the northeastern states, where the drop-off in enrollments is expected to be more severe, may reach catastrophic proportions.

As for the public state colleges, many of them former state teachers' colleges transformed into liberal arts institutions to handle the booming '60s and '70s, their future is mostly in the hands of state legislatures. Confronted by enrollment losses, the lawmakers may decide to continue most of the schools (although reduced in size) and close some. On the other hand, the flagship campuses of the state universities probably face modest losses in enrollment, since they have enjoyed for years an annual surplus of applicants. Similarly, the nationally renowned private colleges and universities should have no real trouble, since they draw students from all parts of the country. Public community colleges are also favorably positioned because of their relatively low tuition and their flexibility in adapting programs to changing needs.

Whether in better or worse position, however, every institution would do well to devote some hard thinking to the shrinking-enrollment dilemma. At best, it will assure continued excellence. At worst, it will offer a better chance to survive. Breneman (1983) suggests key questions for institutions to answer as they plan for and adapt to the future:

1. Is the college's present planning process adequate for the years ahead?
2. How realistic are institutional enrollment projections? How accurate have past projections been?
3. What have been the relationships among enrollment levels, costs, and revenues in recent years? What approximate effect would a 10 or 15 percent decline in enrollment over the next five years have on costs and revenues?
4. What is the student attrition rate from the various degree programs, and how has it changed over time?
5. Is there a case for charging different tuition rates by program or level of study to reflect cost differences more accurately? Should the college match, exceed, or lag behind price increases of its competitors?
6. Should the college seek to attract new client groups to maintain enrollments? If so, what will be the impact on the institution's traditional mission?
7. Given current staffing patterns, how flexible is the college in shifting program direction? Are faculty development and redirection realistic possibilities? At what point, under what circumstances, and with what procedures might it be necessary to dismiss tenured faculty?
8. Are there alternative uses for campus buildings (including dormitories) that are rendered superfluous by a decade or more of enrollment declines? Can these surplus physical assets be converted into revenue producers?
9. At what point will continued deferred maintenance and aging equipment adversely affect enrollment?
10. How dependent has the college become on federal and state student aid? Is it possible to estimate the proportion of the student body that would withdraw if significant cuts were made in grant and loan programs? Can the college realistically plan to replace government aid by support or credit commitments from new sources?

Corporate Educational Institutions

From an unexpected direction looms another threat to college and university solvency. The institutions of higher education face growing competition from corporations moving into the education business. As corporations assumed greater responsibility for the education of their employees, they started their own institutions of higher learning. By mid-1983, more than 400 business sites included a building labeled "college," "university," "institute," or "educational center." In fact, corporate-run education and training programs, costing more than $30 billion annually, became the fastest growing education offshoot in the country.

Many of these new institutions offer the same range of courses — in the subject areas in which they focus — available at traditional colleges. Two thousand two hundred fifty courses offered by more than 140 business and industrial corporations and other organizations are of sufficient quality to merit academic credit, according to the American Council on Education, which evaluates formal educational programs of noncollegiate institutions. To make matters worse, a few of the corporate colleges admit students who are not employees. The institutions cover a wide spectrum of the corporate world. As examples, Watkins (1983c) offers the following:

- The American Telephone and Telegraph Company's National Management Training Center for Technical Education offers programs to more than 30,000 students annually, not all of them employees of AT&T. More than 500 administrators, faculty members, and curriculum specialists are on the center's staff.
- Arthur D. Little's Management Education Institute, a subsidiary of the management-consultant firm, offers a program leading to a master's degree in the science of management. Students pay $11,000 for the eleven-month program, which

includes courses in economics and industrial development, international business, and energy-resource management. The institute is accredited by the New England Association of Schools and Colleges.

- The Wang Institute of Graduate Studies, established by the founder of Wang Laboratories (a computer manufacturer), offers a master's degree in software engineering. The independent, nonprofit education institution is accredited by the New England Association.
- The General Motors Institute offers a bachelor's degree in engineering and industrial administration. Regionally accredited, the institute enrolls 2,300 full-time students, most of whom ranked in the top 10 percent of their high school class.

Some corporations even have campuses for their studying employees. For example, the McDonald Corporation's Hamburger University, in Elk Grove, Illinois, offers courses ranging from fiscal management to human relations. The Xerox Corporation's Center for Training and Management Development, in Leesburg, Virginia, offers a rich curriculum and the latest technology for effective teaching. The Holiday Inn University, in Olive Branch, Mississippi, a sprawling institution, offers courses such as performance evaluation and professional salesmanship. Each provides a campus for students.

In short, the line between the corporate and the college classroom is slowly being obliterated. The monopoly that traditional colleges and universities held on higher education is under challenge as job-based education becomes more appealing to students. In some very significant ways, businessmen and educators appear to be on a collision course.

Why are corporations moving successfully into higher education? The answer seems to be the inadequate response of colleges and universities. Important trends were established in recent years but were perceived differently by educational institutions. First, there was the stimulus to continuing education and re-education in the professions as a result of exploding technologies. Second, there was greater sensitivity to human interaction, which spawned an unprecedented number of human relations programs. Third, a growing throng of men and women re-entered the labor market after a prolonged absence or changed careers, both necessitating retraining. Many colleges and universities saw the handwriting big and clear but misread the message. They interpreted the need in their own image and set up more campus courses, credit hours, and classical curricula. The relatively few institutions venturing into off-campus and/or noncredit programs were in general frowned on and belittled as apostates.

The Hunt for More Money

Plagued by fiscal problems, the nation's colleges and universities began vigorous campaigns to make ends meet. Almost every institution cultivated alumni, wealthy individuals, corporations, foundations, and religious organizations for generous donations. The campaigns succeeded as each segment increased support by as much as 25 percent. In fact, the total voluntary support for the nation's higher education institutions climbed by almost 15 percent, to an estimated $4.86 billion in 1981–82, according to the Council for Financial Aid to Education. In the case of alumni, for example, the council estimated that almost 20 percent contributed to the annual fund appeal in 1981–82, compared to fewer than 17 percent the previous year.

In addition to the traditional methods of fund raising, many colleges and universities went in for the unconventional. They became builders, landlords, and investors in unusual enterprises in a daring effort to raise needed cash.

Park College (Missouri) signed a royalty agreement giving a private company permission to mine limestone beneath the campus. Lake Erie College (Ohio) drilled a well on campus, which paid off spectacularly when the drillers struck natural gas. Nazareth College (Michigan) turned a partly empty dormitory into apartments for the elderly. Biscayne College (Florida) rented its athletic facilities to the Miami Dolphins (football) and the Baltimore Orioles (baseball). Northwood Institute (Michigan) sponsored auctions. Oklahoma Christian College opened an educational amusement park.

A large number of colleges and universities moved into the real estate business, developing multi-million-dollar projects on urban and suburban tracts formerly held in reserve for campus expansion. With enrollment dropping, there seemed less need to hold the land for future campus expansion than to produce revenue by building shopping centers, office buildings, industrial parks, corporate research facilities, hotels, and condominiums. Most of the colleges and universities venturing into the tough real estate–development market formed partnerships with experienced development companies and hired real estate managers and consultants.

Impact on Instructional Staff

Since higher education is a labor-intensive industry, with 70 to 80 percent of most budgets going for salaries, it was inevitable for the instructional staff to be regarded as one of the first areas to be pruned. A large number of colleges and universities neatly avoided the high salaries and fringe benefits of full-time faculty by hiring lower-salaried, few-or-no-benefit, part-time instructors. Between 1970 and 1978, part-time faculty members doubled in numbers, while full-time faculty members increased by 21 percent. Since part-time faculty members could be hired and dismissed to fit the institutions' changing needs, the overall savings to the institutions were considerable.

Other colleges and universities ducked the escalating salaries of senior instructors by employing junior faculty members, who were dropped at the expiration of their short-term contracts, regardless of sterling or mediocre performance. The "gypsy scholars," as they were called, were hired for a year or two, often to replace a professor on leave. They were assigned, however, a full teaching load and expected to do the requisite research and service. But they moved like nomads every year or two from institution to institution, spending much of their time scouring the job market to land the next teaching job. The use of "gypsy scholars" represented savings to the institutions.

In the short term, those institutions choosing to hire part-timers and "gypsy scholars" instead of full-time faculty reduced their costs. In the long term, however, they will probably pay a heavy price as their full-time faculty ages and the institutions lose the synergy derived from the intermixing of older and younger faculty members. The loss of institutional vitality will sap the quality of the institutions.

While colleges and universities were trying to cut costs and increase income, they were constantly on the carpet before community and governmental groups to hold professors accountable for academic performance. State legislatures, which funded the public colleges and universities, took keen interest in discovering how faculty members allocated their time. And boards of trustees of private institutions brought the professional activities of faculty members under close scrutiny.

Some institutions were directed to report on the percentage of professional time and salary devoted to teaching, related administration, and other professional assignments. Other institutions agreed to adopt a budgetary process in which each department head had to justify the continued funding of the salary of each professor and of each program or course in the department. Still other institutions were directed to freeze the granting of tenure and promotion to senior rank. The pressure for teaching accountability reached as high in government as the president of the United States. In a commencement address at Seton Hall University (New Jersey), President Reagan urged that professors be paid and promoted "on the basis of their merit and competence."

The groundswell across the nation for faculty accountability enlisted taxpayers, institutional trustees, financial donors, and students, all of whom pressured colleges and universities to scrutinize each department's cost effectiveness and each professor's performance. Institutions of higher education found themselves under the gun to re-examine the problems associated with promotion and tenure. They had to find ways to separate the wheat from the chaff. Who on the faculty was to be promoted? Who granted tenure? Whose employment terminated?

The clear need was to squeeze hearsay and gossip out of the evaluative process and rely increasingly on objective and substantive data. As a result, almost every college and university moved its evaluative process to the top of its priority list. The movement to improve faculty evaluation procedures soon swept the nation's campuses, where overcrowded seminars and conferences on the subject and sold-out printings of faculty evaluation guidebooks indicated unflagging interest. Almost all colleges and universities sought to compare their faculty evaluation practices with the practices around the country. They wanted to learn why some systems worked and others failed. They wanted to know in advance and overcome the inherent problems in specific programs to make them more objective. And they wanted their appraisal systems to be more responsive to specific procedures stemming from civil rights legislation that directly influences the faculty evaluation process.

Chapter 2

Court Challenges
to Administrative Decisions
on Tenure, Promotion,
and Retention

A serious problem that arises in promotion and tenure decisions in colleges and universities is that these decisions, mostly rendered by peers at the departmental level, are not always guided by objective evidence. No one who has played a long and active role in peer evaluation would deny that academic worth has central importance in these decisions. Unfortunately, politics and personality all too often play a role as well. It is not unknown for a promotion and tenure committee member, even a chairperson, to thumb through personnel files seeking negative information on which to hang an adverse prejudgment.

Today, however, promotion and tenure decisions are no longer private affairs within the department. More and more, they are subject to affirmative action guidelines and courtroom scrutiny. Discrimination complaints in increasing numbers are forcing committee members to publicly justify decisions that formerly were left to their private discretion. What triggered this important change? In 1972, an amendment to Title VII of the Civil Rights Act of 1964 extended that law's prohibition against discrimination in employment for reasons of race, sex, or religion to colleges and universities. Many institutions promptly hired women and minority members for nontenured junior positions. Now, a decade later, many of these women and minority members are being considered for promotion and tenure. And some of the institutions that were prompt to hire them are foot dragging on promotion to senior levels and granting tenure. Some women and minority members, convinced that the unspoken reason is discrimination, file suit. There is, unfortunately, more than casual evidence for this serious charge.

First, a recent study by the prestigious National Research Council found objective factors inadequate to explain salary and academic rank differences between male and female teachers. The study matched 5,164 males and females by education, experience, and teaching field. Second, the National Center for Education Statistics found that 49.9 percent of female professors are tenured, compared with 70 percent of male professors. In 1974, when the center began keeping such statistics, 40.9 percent of the women and 58.4 percent of the men were tenured. Thus, over the years, a greater percentage of men than women were granted tenure. Third, a 1983 study by the American Assembly of Collegiate Schools of Business found that fewer than 15 percent of the faculty in university business schools were women. The study of 400 business schools also found that 9 percent of the faculty were Asian, 4 percent were black, and under 2 percent were Hispanic.

In recent years, the number of discrimination charges leveled at public and private colleges and universities and professional schools has multiplied with near-explosive speed. By 1976, some 3,000 discrimination charges had been filed with the Equal Employment Opportunity Commission (EEOC). Although the EEOC no longer keeps such statistics, a conservative estimate is that the number of charges has tripled. Moreover, these statistics do not include the considerable number of discrimination charges filed with the human rights commissions in the states. Few institutions have been immune. Harvard, Cornell, Princeton, Swarthmore, Fordham, Vanderbilt, Michigan State, Kent State, and the universities of Texas, Oregon, and Minnesota are the better known names among the hundreds of colleges and universities hit by discrimination suits filed by faculty members.

The Right of "Discovery"

The judicial process of "discovery," the right of someone involved in litigation to gather evidence, may require faculty members on promotion and tenure committees to disclose how they voted. This judicial requirement collides with the historical tradition of academic freedom. Most professors are dismayed by and resistant to what they consider an invasion of academic privacy and their right to the secret ballot. They cherish the confidentiality of committee decisions, because it permits individual negative votes without risking anger or challenge to the negative voter by the professor under evaluation. They argue that if the committee is shorn of confidentiality, its free exercise of critical judgment will be impaired.

The Dinnan Case. In June 1982, the U.S. Supreme Court refused to review the celebrated contempt-of-court conviction of James Dinnan, a University of Georgia professor who went to jail rather than reveal how he had voted in a tenure case. The court let stand without comment a ruling by a lower court that the right to academic freedom must be limited by other societal goals. The lower court had upheld the ruling by the district court, where the case had originated. The district judge had found Dinnan in contempt of court for refusing to obey an order to reveal how he had voted when Maija Blaubergs, an assistant professor in his department, was denied tenure.

Blaubergs had charged in a suit that she had been denied tenure and reappointment because of her sex. To develop the case, her lawyer argued the need to know how six of the nine committee members had voted. Five of the six reluctantly complied, but Dinnan refused on the ground that his vote was protected as confidential by both university policy and the U.S. Constitution. The court ruled against him. When Dinnan still refused to comply, he was found in contempt of court, fined $3,000, and sentenced to ninety days in jail. Colleagues helped to pay the fine.

In appealing the case all the way to the Supreme Court, Dinnan hoped to win a ruling that would immunize tenure committee members from legal suit. He insisted that unless their voting anonymity was protected, faculty members would cease serving on tenure committees. He argued also that the integrity of the academic process was at risk if voting confidentiality was breached. But the decision handed down by the three-judge panel concluded: "We find nothing heroic or noble about the appellant's position; we see only an attempt to avoid responsibility for his actions. If the appellant was unwilling to accept responsibility for his actions, he should never have taken part in the tenure decision-making process. However, once he accepted such a role of public trust, he subjected himself to explaining to the public and any affected individual his decisions and the reasons behind them."

The court rejected the idea that professors would be inhibited in making tenure decisions if they had to reveal their votes, saying: "We fail to see how, if a tenure committee is acting in good faith, our decision today will adversely affect its decision-making process. Indeed, this opinion should work to reinforce responsible decision making in tenure questions as it sends out a clear signal to would-be wrongdoers that they may not hide behind 'academic freedom' to avoid responsibility for their actions" ("Text of Appeals-Court Opinions. . . ," 1981, p. 14).

The court thus found that society's stake in due process and affirmative action transcends higher education's stake in academic freedom and confidentiality. The court also made clear that when it came to the protection of individual rights as provided in the U.S. Constitution and in Title VII of the Civil Rights Acts of 1964 and 1972, academia is not immune to the court's jurisdiction.

The Gray Case. Although the decision by committee is always disclosed, the individual votes of the committee members rarely are. It is also uncommon for a professor to be given specific reasons for a negative academic judgment. Some institutions argue that the shroud of silence enveloping a committee decision is best for the professor. In 1967, the Board of Higher Education of the City of New York asserted in a policy statement that giving reasons "is really not in the best interest of the candidate himself, for it makes a matter of record a negative evaluation which may come back to plague him later" ("Personnel and Budget Procedures," 1967, p. 601). A similar position was taken by a large midwestern university when it informed new faculty members: "It shall not be necessary for the dean or department chairman to provide any causes or reasons for not recommending reappointment" (Balch, 1980, p. 26). Unfortunately, it is almost inevitable that silence about a negative decision raises for some professors the suspicion of discrimination.

Shall a professor who requests the information not be told the reasons? The answer to that question is at the heart of the precedent-setting case of *Gray* v. *The City University of New York (LaGuardia Community College)*. After teaching for five years, Professor Gray was denied tenure and reappointment for the 1979–80 academic year at LaGuardia Community College. In his view, the decision was discriminatory, and the black instructor filed suit under the Civil Rights Act. He sought background information on the individual votes of the tenure and reappointment committee. Two members refused, citing academic freedom and confidentiality. District Judge Lawrence Pierce came down on the side of the two committee members, ruling that protecting confidentiality in tenure decisions is essential to preserving academic freedom. Gray appealed the decision.

The court of appeals overturned the ruling and decided that individual members of the committee could be compelled to reveal how they voted as possible evidence that Gray was the victim of racial discrimination. The decision implied that colleges and universities are expected to be more forthright in providing unsuccessful candidates with reasons for their rejection, especially when discrimination is at issue. The court granted Gray's motion because he had received no reasons for his rejection and had therefore been forced to "chase an invisible quarry" in trying to prove discrimination. Moreover, the court held that "academic freedom is illusory when it does not protect faculty from censurious practices but rather serves as a veil for those who might act as censors" (Perry, 1982, p. 18).

The court's decision walked a tightrope between the plaintiff's right of discovery and academia's right of confidentiality. "Rather than adopting a rule of absolute disclosure in reckless disregard of the need for confidentiality," the court said, "or adopting a rule of complete privilege that would frustrate reasonable challenges to the fairness of a hiring decision, our statement today

holds that absent a statement of reasons, the balance tips toward discovery and away from recognition of privilege" (p. 18). The court acknowledged that, in its deliberations, it had relied on policies of the American Association of University Professors (AAUP), which seek to protect confidentiality in tenure decisions and simultaneously to support the right of professors to a written explanation of an adverse decision. The AAUP position "strikes an appropriate balance between academic freedom and educational excellence, on the one hand, and individual rights to fair consideration, on the other," the court said (p. 18). In 1971, the AAUP promulgated a position paper that called for written explanations to professors who were denied promotion. This policy, the court found, "may serve to avoid arbitrariness."

The *Dinnan* and *Gray* cases have been closely monitored in higher education circles around the nation, both for clues to the fate of thousands of discrimination cases now in the courts and for further evidence that the courts are departing from the traditional reluctance to inject themselves into academic decisions.

Establishing Assessment Criteria

Historically, the courts have exhibited a distaste for overturning administrative decisions unless arbitrarily, capriciously, or irrelevantly based. The underlying assumption is that due process is served unless the evidence against that assumption is overwhelming. Thus, the courts are generally disinterested in the particular methods or criteria employed in faculty evaluation. Kaplin (1978, p. 129) finds that the courts are "less likely to become involved in disputes concerning the substance of standards and criteria than in disputes over procedures for enforcing standards and criteria." Specifically, as to sources of information, types of ratings, and relative weights assigned to criteria in promotion or tenure decisions, the courts are generally loath to supplant academic judgments with judicial judgments.

A case in point is *Labat* v. *Board of Higher Education, City University of New York* (1975) in which Judge Edward Weinfeld decided that "the weight to be given scholarly writings . . . in a tenure decision involves judgmental evaluations by those who live in

the academic world. [Assessment of] scholarship and research should be left to scholars" (Holley and Feild, 1977, p. 438).

Along the same lines, in *Goolsby* v. *Regents of University of Georgia* (Civil Action No. C-11236 Super. Ct. Fulton County, Georgia, (1976)), the presiding judge ruled that the criteria used "in performance evaluation relating to professors' promotions and salary increases involve judgmental decisions which are, at best, difficult and in the court's opinion are best left to those entrusted to make the same, i.e., college administrators." And in *Green* v. *Board of Regents, Texas Tech University* (1971), the court of appeals judge concluded that to evaluate the criteria selected by the university was necessarily judgmental and refused to substitute a judicial judgment for that of the educational experts (Holley and Feild, 1977, p. 439).

While the courts generally stay out of the methods-and-criteria arena in the judging of faculty performance, they show no such reluctance in three other kinds of dispute. First, when the evaluation criteria are in the faculty handbook or are in the institution's by-laws, they are considered part of the legal contract between the institution and the faculty member. In a dispute over the application of the criteria, the courts will intervene. For example, if student evaluation is listed in the faculty handbook as part of the evaluation procedure and is omitted in practice, a suit can properly ensue. Second, when the evaluation criteria lack specificity and/or are not job-related, the courts will intervene. For example, tenure cannot properly be denied to a professor on the basis of appearance or sense of humor. Third, the courts will intervene when a complaint of discrimination is filed against an institution under the various federal and/or state statutes. The governmental agencies charged with enforcement are concerned with all the institution's considerations that led to its tenure-promotion-dismissal decision.

To overcome a charge of race, sex, or ethnic discrimination, an institution of higher education must demonstrate that the evaluation measurements meet acceptable validity levels and that discrimination played no part in the decision. Hollander, in the *Legal Handbook for Educators* (1978), underscores the point that courts are reluctant to overrule decisions of administrators and faculty members but will intervene when the institution neglects to obey its own rules or acts arbitrarily or capriciously.

Establishing a Prima Facie Case

Under Title VII of the Civil Rights Act, the aggrieved professor has the initial burden of presenting prima facie evidence of a specific discriminatory act. One way to establish such evidence is to demonstrate that the criteria used to evaluate performance are unevenly applied, biased, and fatally subjective. Another is to demonstrate the statistical disparity of male and female professors, at, for example, associate professor rank. Once a prima facie case is established, the burden of proof shifts to the institution, which must present nondiscriminatory reasons to explain away the charge.

Although most discrimination suits are filed under Title VII of the Civil Rights Act, some are brought under the due process clause of the Fifth Amendment and a few under the equal protection clause of the Fourteenth Amendment. The suits filed on constitutional grounds impose on the complainant the heavy burden of showing "intent to discriminate," which is not required under Title VII. In the latter case, only the result, the impact, of a challenged promotion or tenure practice needs to be shown. Since "intent to discriminate" is far more difficult to prove than "impact," it is probable that most discrimination cases will continue to be filed under Title VII.

Uniform Guidelines on Employee Selection Procedures

The Equal Employment Opportunity Commission, created by the federal government to put teeth into Title VII, has published a series of guidelines (*Uniform Guidelines on Employee Selection Procedures*, 1978) to provide factual information to those involved in the selection and evaluation of personnel. Since the guidelines are utilized by the courts in resolving promotion and tenure disputes, they should be carefully studied, understood, and followed, in both spirit and letter, to avert even the suspicion of discrimination. The guidelines apply to all methods used to make personnel decisions, including written tests, interviews, work samples, and performance ratings.

Whichever method is used, because of possible adverse effects on race, sex, or ethnic groups, it should be validated in accord with the guidelines whenever possible. Although validation is always desirable, the guidelines mandate it only when a method adversely affects the opportunities of a race, sex, or ethnic group. If one group receives generally lower student ratings, for example, a member of that group can claim that the ratings unduly biased his or her opportunity for promotion. The institution would then have to demonstrate the validity of the ratings as an assessment of job performance. The evidence needed to defend the validity of the assessment method should be considered before the method is implemented. Any rating scale or evaluation system that includes criteria irrelevant to the job (for example, neatness) is probably headed for trouble in court.

A word of caution may be in order for faculty members on promotion and tenure committees and for administrators of performance evaluation systems. They should be alert to flawed decisions that are open to legal suit. Discrimination can be soiling to both the institution and the victim. Today, colleges and universities increasingly rely on legal counsel to help formulate institutional policies and to prepare legal defenses for personnel decisions.

Settling Out of Court

With the multiplication of court cases in recent years has come a like multiplication of discrimination cases settled out of court. The reasons? Fear that the case will be lost in court, the desire to avoid paying high legal fees, and a distaste for the unpleasant publicity that inevitably accompanies a public charge of discrimination. There is another reason to settle out of court — the institution need admit to no wrongdoing as part of the settlement. The following cases were reported in a few months in early 1983 by *The Chronicle of Higher Education* as settled out of court:

• The University of the District of Columbia agreed to promote a Hispanic faculty member from associate to full professor and provide him with $11,500 in back pay ("University of the District of Columbia...," 1983).

- Fordham University (New York) agreed to an undisclosed cash settlement with a Protestant theologian who accused the university of denying him tenure because of his religion ("Theologian Denied Tenure . . . ," 1983).
- The University of Minnesota agreed to pay thirty-seven female librarians $750,000 in back pay and fringe benefits in a sex-discrimination settlement ("Thirty-seven Women Settle Case . . . ," 1983).
- The University of Oregon agreed to rehire its former director of affirmative action and pay her $50,000 to settle her charge of race and sex discrimination ("University of Oregon Rehires . . . ," 1983).

Two precedent-setting tenure discrimination cases involving gender were settled out of court several years ago (Jackson, 1983, p. 17). The University of Minnesota agreed to pay a large compensatory award and to hire women to fill two of the next five faculty positions in the chemistry department. Brown University agreed to award tenure retroactively to three female faculty members and to set up a $400,000 fund to pay damages to other women found to have been discriminated against.

Recent Court Decisions

The courts in recent years have ruled many colleges and universities in violation of law in an array of decisions and penalties. Some institutions have been ordered by the courts to reverse personnel judgments. For example, a federal appellate court in 1980 ordered Muhlenberg College (Pennsylvania) to award tenure to a physical education professor after finding that she was turned down because of her sex (Fiske, 1983).

Other institutions have been ordered to pay damages and court costs. In 1983, for example, a federal judge ruled that the University of Texas at El Paso discriminated against a female assistant professor of mathematics by paying her less than males with similar backgrounds and teaching comparable courses in the same department ("Math Professor . . . ," 1983). The judge awarded the plaintiff $15,428 in damages and ordered the university to pay her legal fees. In his decision, the judge observed that the university disregarded its own policy, which mandated promotion or dismissal after seven years, by keeping the plaintiff at the same level for fourteen years. The court refused to accept the defendant's explanation that "it simply forgot" to promote her for seven years. In another 1983 case, Tufts University (Massachusetts) was ordered to pay more than $350,000 to a former faculty member who was denied tenure ("Former Professor at Tufts...," 1983). The ruling came in a lawsuit filed by a professor who charged the university with breach of contract and misrepresentation. She maintained that she had not been told when she was hired that the administration had decided it would no longer award tenure to members of her department. At this writing, university officials are undecided whether to appeal the decision.

Still other institutions have been found guilty of discrimination in class-action suits affecting as many as 10,000 past and present employees. In 1983, for example, a federal district judge ruled that the City University of New York had discriminated against female teachers for fifteen years by paying them less than males in equivalent positions (McFadden, 1983). Back pay and damage awards for the thousands of women affected were not incorporated into the decision and at this writing are still to be fixed. But legal experts estimate the figure in millions of dollars. The judge's decision was based largely on a statistical analysis of salaries. The difference in the average annual salary between men and women was $1,800. The class-action suit, filed in 1973 by twenty-five women employed at the university's seventeen senior and community colleges, charged the university with discrimination in salaries, hiring, promotion, and fringe benefits. The judge's decision addressed only the issue of salaries. University officials at this writing are undecided whether to appeal the judge's decision.

In another suit charging sex bias in the fixing of salaries, a federal district court in Oregon ruled that Western Oregon State College violated the law by paying lower salaries to females than to males in its education and physical education departments (Fields, 1983, p. 14). A statistician testifying for the plaintiffs calculated the statistical probability that the salary disparity could happen by chance was one in a hundred. The court ruled that the institution knew of the disparity and willfully violated the Equal Pay Act. The court's decision was appealed on the ground that the

Equal Pay Act does not prohibit the hiring of highly qualified persons and paying commensurately higher salaries so long as the employer would pay the same amount to males or females.

What separates this case from others like it, however, is the filing of "friend of the court" briefs by third parties with vital stakes in the legal outcome. The brief filed by the American Council on Education, for example, argued against the district court's decision. "The clear message to institutions," said the council, "would be that all teachers of a given rank must be paid the same salary, regardless of the department in which they teach, their market value, their skills and experiences, and their seniority." In addition, the brief criticized the lower court for ignoring some situations in which women were paid more than men with similar jobs.

A different viewpoint was offered in the "friend of the court" brief filed by the Women's Equity Action League. It argued that the lower court's decision "does not mean that all college teachers must be paid identically. The law requires, however, that schools use consistent, understandable, nondiscriminatory factors in setting faculty wages. To argue otherwise is to claim a special privilege for colleges and universities to discriminate." The brief also noted that when Congress amended the Equal Pay Act in 1972 to cover professional employees at colleges and universities, it acted because widespread bias against female employees had been revealed in congressional hearings. The case is being closely watched as a potential bellwether in sex-discrimination suits.

In recent years, some court decisions have found for colleges and universities. For example, the U.S. Supreme Court refused to reconsider a lower court's ruling that the University of Texas Health Science Center at Houston was not guilty of sex bias when it refused to promote a female assistant professor of medicine to an associate professorship ("Court Refuses to Review . . . ," 1983). The lower court had ruled that the institution had produced adequate evidence that its refusal to promote the plaintiff was due to insufficient publication and teaching experience at the graduate level, among other reasons.

A federal district judge ruled that Cornell University was not guilty of sex bias when it denied tenure to five former female faculty members. The judge found the university's reasons for the denial nondiscriminatory. The five women simply did not meet

Cornell's rigorous standard for tenure, he said ("In Brief," 1983, p. 2). In another recent and widely publicized case, the U.S. Supreme Court declined to review a lower court's decision upholding Michigan State University's denial of tenure to a teacher in its Latin American Center ("Professor Asks Supreme Court to Review...," 1982). The teacher claimed that the institution failed to use normal review procedures when it refused him tenure. The lower court, in setting aside a jury's verdict for the teacher, ruled that the university's denial was for constitutionally permissible reasons.

An overview of recent court decisions does not seem to produce a consistently uniform body of law in discrimination cases. But from the many hundreds of discrimination cases being filed against colleges and universities, precedents are clearly in the process of being established. It is no more than prudent, therefore, for colleges and universities to review their hiring, promotion, and tenure procedures to eliminate any existing inequities before they are aired in court.

Constitutional Due Process

Colleges and universities reviewing their evaluation practices should give full attention to due process. Constitutional due process means following certain principles, such as providing faculty members with proper notice and an opportunity for a fair hearing. The application of due process to faculty evaluations is more than desirable; it is perceived as the faculty member's right. It is provided to faculty members, as to all citizens, under the Fourteenth Amendment, which says that states shall not deprive any person of life, liberty, or property without due process of law. The property and liberty guaranteed by the Fourteenth Amendment are being applied by the courts today not only to public institutions but increasingly also to private institutions of higher education. Almost all private institutions receive some state or federal funding, which opens them additionally to court scrutiny.

Briefly, then, colleges and universities must provide procedural safeguards to faculty members whenever personnel decisions infringe on the members' property or liberty. For example, decisions to terminate faculty who are tenured or in mid-contract must be accompanied by such procedural safeguards, since the decisions clearly have an impact on property interests.

Kaplin (1978, pp. 136–137) reports that nonrenewal of a faculty appointment requires appropriate safeguards particularly if "(1) The existing rules, policies or practices of the institution, or mutually 'explicit understandings' between the faculty member and the institution, support the faculty member's claim of entitlement to continued employment; (2) the institution, in the course of nonrenewal, makes charges against the faculty member that could seriously damage his or her reputation, standing, or association in the community; (3) the nonrenewal imposes a 'stigma or other disability' on the faculty member that forecloses his or her freedom to take advantage of other employment opportunities."

Where specific personnel procedures exist, the courts have been inclined to require faculty members to exhaust all internal procedures before filing suit. Therefore, if institutions follow their written procedures, in letter and spirit, and provide compelling evidence to that effect, they are on firm legal ground. But when they depart from their own procedures, they become sitting ducks for suits and judicial condemnation.

In *Nzomo* v. *Vermont State Colleges* (1978), for example, the institution's written faculty evaluation rules called for (1) the division directors and the department chair to discuss their recommendations with the faculty member and (2) the recommendations then to be brought to the president's advisory committee on promotion/ tenure (Centra, 1979, p. 139). The college's failure to follow its written procedures led the Supreme Court of Vermont to rule that the contractual relationship between the college and the professor had been violated.

Which due process rights of a faculty member must be protected before tenure is denied? A West Virginia court (*McLendon* v. *Morton* (1978) provided an answer. As Kaplin (1980, pp. 57–58) describes the case:

Parkersburg Community College published eligibility criteria for tenure, which included six years as a teaching member of the full-time faculty and attainment of the rank of assistant professor.

Having fulfilled both criteria, McLendon applied for tenure. After her tenure application was rejected, McLendon filed suit, claiming that the institution's failure to provide her a hearing abridged her due process rights.

The court held that (1) satisfying objective eligibility standards gave McLendon sufficient entitlement, so that she could not be denied tenure without some procedural due process; and (2) minimal due process necessitates notice of the reasons for denial and a hearing before an unbiased tribunal, at which the professor can refute the issues raised in the notice.

In West Virginia and other jurisdictions that accept the *McLendon* reasoning, institutions must provide notice and an opportunity for a hearing before a decision denying tenure. If a faculty member is tenured, which due process procedures must be followed by the institution before it can dismiss him or her? Citing the case of *Poterma* v. *Ping* (1978), Kaplin (1980, p. 57) suggests an answer.

A tenured member of the Economics Department at Ohio University claimed that he was denied due process when the university dismissed him for failure to perform his faculty duties and inability to communicate with students.

The court ruled that the minimum due process safeguards included: (1) a written statement of the reasons for the proposed termination prior to final action, (2) adequate notice of a hearing, (3) a hearing at which the teacher has an opportunity to submit evidence to contravert the grounds for dismissal, (4) a final statement of the grounds for dismissal if it does occur.

The court held that the university had complied with these requirements and had not infringed the faculty member's due process rights.

Establishing faculty evaluation procedures to provide due process demands time and effort, but once such procedures are established, more disputes can be resolved by internal dialogue and conciliation than by the lengthy, expensive adversarial process of the courts. There is no doubt that colleges and universities generally wish to be fair in faculty tenure, promotion, and retention decisions; due process built into the procedures helps to guarantee that fairness. As Polishook (1982, p. 91) wrote: "By conforming to basic principles of evidence, by allowing the individual to participate in the common effort to reach an accurate appraisal, by attempting to guard against. . . subjectivity, due process assures an accurate conclusion." Actually, the autonomy that colleges and universities claim over their own governance is more likely to be breached if the institutions' due process procedures can be faulted by faculty members. Thus, due process plays an indispensable role even in the institutions' autonomy.

No one would care to argue that all disputes within the evaluation process are finally resolvable within the institution and that the disparate interests of the institution, the professor, and society can always be orchestrated without ever resorting to the courts. But a few basic safeguards can go a long way to bring the impossible at least closer. First, the improvement function of faculty evaluation must be divorced from the personnel-decision function. Both aspects of faculty evaluation are of vital importance, but they must be kept separate. As Polishook (1982, p. 98) states: "An individual who ingenuously submits to criticism in hope of professional advancement may also create devastating initial impressions that are sometimes insurmountable; such a professor is placed at great disadvantage during every year of evaluation." Second, due process demands more than lip service; it must be incorporated in the evaluation procedures and scrupulously adhered to in letter and spirit in practice. Among other requirements, due process should include (1) written and publicized criteria for retention, promotion, and tenure decisions; (2) a well-defined appeal procedure; (3) an understanding, accepted by faculty and administration, of the circumstances under which the institution's management will overturn peer committee judgments; (4) a fair and evenhanded approach to faculty appraisal; (5) strict reliance on the rules of evidence in reaching personnel decisions; and (6) a statement of reasons provided to the faculty member for a negative decision. Altogether, meticulous adherence to these criteria should assure faculty members of careful, objective weighing of their performance and arrival at a just decision.

Checklist for Faculty Evaluation Programs

The following suggested checklist was developed from a review of recent court cases, the EEOC guidelines, and the current literature on legal aspects of faculty evaluation.

1. Personnel decisions must not be discriminatory in intent, application, or results.
2. All parts of the evaluation program must be job related and subject to empirical validation.
3. Administrators, especially department chairs, must have current and accurate knowledge about the rights and responsibilities of colleges and universities relative to faculty evaluation.
4. The criteria and procedures in the evaluation program must be provided in writing and in detail to all faculty members.
5. The criteria and procedures must be followed in spirit and letter.
6. Evaluation forms must be in clear and concise language.
7. Multiple evaluation sources must be employed and each source pursued independently.
8. Evaluators must be adequately trained in the use of evaluation instruments.
9. Administration and scoring of evaluations must be standardized.
10. Evaluations must be conducted in their entirety before reaching personnel decisions.
11. Hearsay is impermissible as evidence in tenure, promotion, or retention decisions.
12. Faculty members must have the opportunity to respond in writing as to the accuracy, relevance, and completeness of their evaluations.
13. Faculty members must be evaluated in accordance with established performance standards and the actual work assigned.
14. Evaluation results must be promptly given to faculty members.
15. Specific and valid reasons must be provided in writing to faculty members who are given negative decisions.
16. A formal appeals system must be part of the evaluation program.
17. Institutions must obtain maximum available insurance as protection against administrative liability in the event of suit.

18. Institutions must employ legal counsel with solid and current knowledge of affirmative action and EEOC guidelines.
19. Legal counsel must keep administrators and faculty informed of their current rights and responsibilities in evaluations.
20. Evaluation programs must have no bias and no appearance of bias.

Institutions following the above suggested guidelines are offered no ironclad guarantee, of course, that they will not be sued, but the possibility of that unpleasant eventuality will be severely reduced. On the positive side, the evaluation systems will incline more toward the improvement and reward of faculty performance, where they properly belong.

Chapter 3

Current Policies and Practices in Evaluating Teaching, Research, and Service:
A New Nationwide Study

Early in 1983, the writer conducted a nationwide survey that disclosed the policies and practices in operation on campuses, how they are changing, and the national trends they indicate. Specifically, the survey's threefold purpose was (1) to examine the wide range of practices and emerging trends in the evaluation of faculty performance, (2) to suggest which practices are in need of improvement, and (3) to provide colleges and universities with comparative data to open the door to improvement in evaluation procedures.

Procedure

First, a word about method. To achieve wide coverage, all the accredited, four-year, undergraduate, liberal arts colleges listed in the U.S. Department of Education's *Educational Directory* for 1981–82 were surveyed. University-related liberal arts colleges were excluded from the study to pare the population to more manageable size. Table 1 illustrates the number and percentage of institutions included in the analysis.

A questionnaire was mailed to 770 academic deans, and within a few weeks, 616 responded. (A copy of the questionnaire

Table 1. Number and Percentage of Institutions
Included in the Analysis, 1983.

Type of Institution	Number Included	Percentage
Private liberal arts college	515	83.6
Public liberal arts college	96	15.6
Unspecified as private or public	5	0.8
Total	616	100

appears in the Appendix.) This unusually high (80 percent) and rapid response suggests the seriousness with which the deans viewed the problems implicit in evaluating faculty performance. Not only did the deans promptly return their filled-in questionnaires, but also many deans sent along faculty manuals, committee reports, and evaluation forms currently in use at their colleges. The miscellany accompanying the questionnaires defied coding, but everything was carefully read, and the impressions gained from this reading are included in this report.

A word also about the genealogy of the questionnaire. It was first developed and used by the American Council on Education in 1967 and was subjected to later revisions by the Educational Testing Service in 1977 and by myself in 1978. It was designed to gather information about current policies and practices of institutions in their evaluation of faculty performance in connection with tenure, promotion in rank, salary increase, and retention.

Each question about the evaluation of overall faculty performance and assessment of college service in the questionnaire called for an answer on a four-point scale: (1) major factor; (2) minor factor; (3) not a factor; (4) not applicable. Each question about the evaluation of teaching or research/scholarship in the questionnaire called for an answer on a different four-point scale: (1) always used; (2) usually used; (3) seldom used; (4) never used. The answers were tallied, and, when appropriate, t-tests were computed to look into response differences.

The questions and the four-point scales were identical to those employed in earlier studies by the writer. It should also be noted that certain changes in population have taken place since the earlier 1978 study. For example, some institutions have since been accredited; a handful have closed or been merged with other institutions. But the number of such institutions is so small that their influence is negligible when it comes to measuring the major changes and trends between the 1978 study and the current one.

The study's findings are divided for clarity into four main sections, each containing numerous tables worthy of detailed scrutiny: (1) evaluating overall faculty performance; (2) evaluating classroom teaching; (3) evaluating scholarship/research; and (4) evaluating college service.

Evaluating Overall Faculty Performance: Findings

When the time comes to consider a faculty member for promotion in rank, tenure, or retention, colleges today choose and weigh a wide range of factors. The questionnaire offered the academic deans thirteen criteria in connection with the evaluation of overall faculty performance. Table 2 shows the academic deans' responses to each factor as a "major factor" or "not a factor." Almost by acclamation, the academic deans chose classroom teaching as the most important index of faculty performance. In private colleges, student advising finished more than 30 percentage points behind the front runner. In public colleges, campus committee work was even more laggard, finishing more than 40 percentage points behind, in second place.

A caution is in order. Please note that although classroom teaching ran away as the most important factor in faculty performance, other factors were not neglected. Academic deans in both private and public colleges consider other professional activity also of major importance. For example, seven additional activities weigh in as "major factors" by at least 20 percent of the private college deans, and seven additional activities receive such designation by 20 percent of the public college deans.

Table 2 points up a number of differences between private and public liberal arts colleges in assessing faculty performance.

Table 2. Frequency of Use of Factors Considered in
Evaluating Overall Faculty Performance in
Liberal Arts Colleges, 1983

| | Private Colleges (N = 515) | | Public Colleges (N = 96) | |
| | Major Factor % | Not a Factor % | Major Factor % | Not a Factor % |
Factors				
Classroom teaching	98.8	0.4	99.0	0.0
Supervision of graduate study	3.1	7.8	7.3	5.2
Supervision of honors program	1.9	17.1	2.1	22.9
Research	31.3	7.0	45.8	2.1
Publication	27.0	6.6	40.6	3.1
Public service	13.8	10.9	35.4	1.0
Consultation (government, business)	1.9	36.1	5.2	26.0
Activity in professional societies	22.3	5.4	34.4	2.1
Student advising	64.9	1.4	43.8	6.3
Campus committee work	52.2	1.2	54.2	2.1
Length of service in rank	48.3	10.1	37.5	15.6
Competing job offers	1.7	64.7	2.1	59.4
Personal attributes	30.7	13.8	15.6	25.0

Private colleges accord greater importance to personal attributes, length of service in rank, and student advising than do public institutions. It comes as no surprise that public colleges, given the public nature of their funding, put a premium on such visible activities as research, publication, public service, and professional society activity. There are a few surprises, however, in Table 2. Differences turn up not only between the private and public liberal arts colleges but also within each group. For example, 30.7 percent of the private college deans considered personal attributes a "major factor," but 13.8 percent dismissed it as "not a factor." Similarly, 15.6 percent of the public college deans viewed personal atrributes as a "major factor," but 25 percent called it "not a factor."

In an analysis of the responses from another vantage point, numerical weights were assigned so that "major factor" carried a one, "minor factor" a two, and "not a factor" (or "not applicable") a three. This method of weighted ratings yields a reasonably accurate picture. Weights of each factor were added, and the sum was divided by the number of responses to yield an arithmetic mean for each. Then, within each category (private or public liberal arts college), factors were ranked in terms of mean scores, a rank of one being assigned to the factor with the lowest mean, a thirteen to the factor with the highest. Thus, the lower the mean, the greater the importance put on that factor by the deans in assessing overall faculty performance. This ranking process, applied by the American Council on Education in an earlier faculty evaluation study, simplifies the process of identifying the most important factors.

Table 3 summarizes the relative importance of the thirteen factors, as the academic deans see them. As mentioned, classroom teaching is the runaway favorite in private and public colleges as a factor in overall faculty performance. Its exceptionally low mean

Table 3. Mean and Rank of Factors Considered in Evaluating Overall Faculty Performance in Liberal Arts Colleges, 1983.

Factors	Private Colleges (N = 515)		Public Colleges (N = 96)		Total (N = 616)[a]	
	Mean	Rank	Mean	Rank	Mean	Rank
Classroom teaching	1.02	1	1.00	1	1.01	1
Supervision of graduate study	2.23	10	1.96	9	2.14	10
Supervision of honors program	2.36	11	2.36	12	2.36	11
Research	1.75	5	1.53	3	1.71	5
Publication	1.79	6	1.63	5	1.76	6
Public service	1.97	9	1.65	6	1.92	9
Consultation (government, business)	2.39	12	2.23	11	2.36	11
Activity in professional societies	1.83	8	1.67	7	1.80	7
Student advising	1.36	2	1.62	4	1.40	2
Campus committee work	1.49	3	1.47	2	1.49	3
Length of service in rank	1.61	4	1.77	8	1.63	4
Competing job offers	2.73	13	2.66	13	2.72	13
Personal attributes	1.82	7	2.11	10	1.86	8

[a]Includes five colleges not specified as private or public.

scores are compelling evidence of its prime importance on almost every liberal arts college campus. Near the bottom of the list for both private and public colleges are consultation, supervision of honors programs, and competing job offers.

Private and public colleges differ sharply, however, in their definitions of academic success. Such benchmarks as research, publication, public service, and activity in professional societies continue to be venerated in public colleges. But the financially squeezed private colleges view student advising (and, by implication, higher student retention rates) of vital importance. The professor's most valuable contribution to his or her institution seems to be to keep students contented and in school. This was underlined by comments from many private college deans. A California dean, for example, wrote: "On our campus, student advising is taken very seriously. We look hard at this area in evaluating our professors. Effective student advising is almost as important as effective teaching. We need both to survive in these hard times." In a similar vein, a Massachusetts dean wrote: "We cannot afford to be concerned with publish-or-perish. If we don't do an effective job in providing students with solid academic advising, the institution itself will perish."

Public colleges, on the contrary, with their expanding proportion of the college population, have diminished student advising to a role of lesser importance than even campus committee work and research. In the words of a public college dean in New York, "Student advising is still important here, but not nearly as important as faculty research." And a Texas dean wrote: "The state legislature looks at the research and publication record of our faculty. Student advising is considered a less important faculty activity."

Table 4 summarizes the relative importance given by academic deans to "major factors" in evaluating overall faculty performance in 1978 and 1983. Even a cursory examination reveals changes, a few quite substantial, between 1978 and 1983. Of the thirteen factors, seven have significantly shifted in importance in the minds of academic deans. Five of the seven have gained in importance: research, publication, public service, activity in professional societies, and campus committee work. Two of the seven

Table 4. Frequency of Use of Factors Considered in
Evaluating Overall Faculty Performance in
Liberal Arts Colleges, 1978 and 1983.

Factors	1978 (N = 680) Major Factor %	1983 (N = 616) Major Factor %
Classroom teaching	98.8	98.7
Supervision of graduate study	2.2	3.7
Supervision of honors program	2.5	1.9
Research	24.5	33.4
Publication	19.0	29.2
Public service	13.7	17.4
Consultation (government, business)	1.2	2.4
Activity in professional societies	17.0	24.5
Student advising	66.7	61.7
Campus committee work	48.8	52.6
Length of service in rank	49.9	46.8
Competing job offers	3.1	1.8
Personal attributes	38.4	28.6

have diminished in importance: student advising and personal attributes. The biggest jump in importance is recorded in research and publication. The biggest slump is in personal attributes.

These changes in the way overall faculty performance is evaluated are underscored in Table 5, which reports t-tests of differences in mean scores of factors considered in performance assessment. The data indicate significant differences at the 0.01 level of confidence between the 1978 and 1983 mean scores of four factors — research, publication, activity in professional societies, and personal attributes. In addition, the difference in the mean scores of one factor — student advising — is significant at the 0.05 level. The mean scores were calculated by adding the assigned numerical weights for each factor (as previously described) and then dividing the sum by the number of responses, to yield an arithmetic mean for each. In most cases, the mean scores obtained in 1983 are lower than those obtained in the earlier study. This suggests that greater importance is being given to more factors in an attempt to cast a wider net and gain greater reliability and range of information in assessing overall faculty performance. It is also quite pos-

Table 5. T-Tests of Differences in Mean Scores of Factors
Considered in Evaluating Overall Faculty Performance
in Liberal Arts Colleges, 1978 and 1983.

Factors	1978 (N = 680) Mean Score	1983 (N = 616) Mean Score	t^a
Classroom teaching	1.01	1.01	− 0.87
Supervision of graduate study	2.26	2.14	1.77
Supervision of honors program	2.36	2.36	0.06
Research	1.83	1.71	3.68[b]
Publication	1.89	1.76	4.30[b]
Public service	1.96	1.92	1.40
Consultation (government, business)	2.41	2.36	1.58
Activity in professional societies	1.88	1.80	2.79[b]
Student advising	1.34	1.40	− 2.00[c]
Campus committee work	1.52	1.49	1.38
Length of service in rank	1.57	1.63	− 1.62
Competing job offers	2.69	2.72	− 0.81
Personal attributes	2.69	1.86	− 3.22[b]
Total mean	1.88	1.85	

[a]The test used was a t-test for differences in independent proportions.
[b]Significant at 0.01 level of confidence.
[c]Significant at 0.05 level of confidence.

sible that wider nets are being cast by academic deans not necessarily to be fair to faculty but to build more comprehensive cases that are less likely to be challenged in court.

Ten years ago, the writer surveyed the policies and practices used by private colleges to evaluate faculty performance (Seldin, 1975a). The report came up with the disheartening finding that many private colleges demonstrated an unwillingness or inability, or both, to develop adequate and equitable methods for faculty evaluation. In the past ten years, some private colleges have been accredited, a few have closed or merged, but the base remains substantially the same and permits comparisons. (Similar base data for public colleges are, unfortunately, unavailable.)

Table 6 reports tests of differences in mean scores of factors considered in overall evaluations in 1973 and 1983. Examination of Table 6 reveals considerable change. In fact, there is statistically significant difference at the 0.01 level between the mean scores of seven of the thirteen factors. And four of the seven

Table 6. T-Tests of Differences in Mean Scores of Factors
Considered in Evaluating Overall Faculty Performance in
Private Liberal Arts Colleges, 1973 and 1983.

Factors	1973 (N = 410) Mean Score	1983 (N = 515) Mean Score	t^a
Classroom teaching	1.01	1.02	– 0.98
Supervision of graduate study	2.17	2.23	– 0.47
Supervision of honors program	2.34	2.36	– 0.27
Research	1.90	1.75	3.83[b]
Publication	1.93	1.79	3.97[b]
Public service	2.01	1.97	1.09
Consultation (government, business)	2.47	2.39	2.37[b]
Activity in professional societies	1.93	1.83	3.01[b]
Student advising	1.34	1.36	– 0.63
Campus committee work	1.51	1.49	0.72
Length of service in rank	1.48	1.61	– 2.89[b]
Competing job offers	2.58	2.73	– 3.92[b]
Personal attributes	1.51	1.82	– 7.31[b]

[a]The test was a t-test for differences in independent proportions.
[b]Significant at 0.01 level of confidence.

factors—research, publication, activity in professional societies, and consultation—have substantially lower mean scores today, indicating their greater importance today. The other three factors—length of service in rank, competing job offers, and personal attributes—have higher means, indicating their decline in importance since the 1973 study.

When did these changes occur? Table 7, reporting how private college academic deans viewed "major factors" in evaluating overall faculty performance in 1973, 1978, and 1983, provides the answer. Six of the seven factors—research, publication, public service, activity in professional societies, length of service in rank, and competing job offers—that reveal statistically significant change in the last ten years show accelerated change between 1978 and 1983. Only one factor—personal attributes—shows more change between 1973 and 1978 than between 1978 and 1983. It dropped as a "major factor" from 53.2 percent in 1973 to 41.1 percent in 1978 and to 30.7 percent in 1983. This continued decline in importance of personal attributes in the minds of academic deans in private liberal arts colleges suggests that their

**Table 7. Frequency of Use of Factors Considered in
Evaluating Overall Faculty Performance in Private
Liberal Arts Colleges, 1973, 1978, and 1983.**

Factors	1973 (N = 410) Major Factor %	1978 (N = 567) Major Factor %	1983 (N = 515) Major Factor %
Classroom teaching	99.3	98.6	98.8
Supervision of graduate study	1.9	1.8	3.1
Supervision of honors program	2.9	2.3	1.9
Research	22.2	22.9	31.3
Publication	17.1	17.3	27.0
Public service	12.9	10.9	13.8
Consultation (government, business)	0.7	1.1	1.9
Activity in professional societies	15.8	16.6	22.3
Student advising	68.8	68.8	64.9
Campus committee work	49.5	51.0	52.2
Length of service in rank	54.4	52.9	48.3
Competing job offers	3.2	3.4	1.7
Personal attributes	53.2	41.1	30.7

faculty will be less prone to administrative criticism for the wrong politics, wrong dress, or wrong friends. As the dean of a private liberal arts college in Florida wrote: "Personal attributes are just not that important any more. Today we are more concerned with whether the faculty member can teach effectively than we are with whether he dresses neatly." Another explanation of far-reaching significance for the possible demise of personal attributes as a "major factor" was offered by an Ohio dean: "Through bitter courtroom experience we've learned that personal attributes won't stand up as the reason to deny a professor tenure. The judge insisted on hard data, but all we could offer were comments about personal attributes. We lost the case."

If private liberal arts colleges have modified the yardsticks they use in evaluating overall faculty performance, so have their public counterparts. Table 8 shows the frequency with which academic deans in public liberal arts colleges used "major factors" in faculty evaluation in 1978 and 1983. Four of the thirteen factors have jumped by ten percentage points or more in the past five years—research, publication, activity in professional societies, and campus committee work. Student advising dropped as a "major

Table 8. Frequency of Use of Factors Considered in
Evaluating Overall Faculty Performance in
Public Liberal Arts Colleges, 1978 and 1983.

Factors	1978 (N = 103) Major Factor %	1983 (N = 96) Major Factor %
Classroom teaching	100.0	99.0
Supervision of graduate study	4.9	7.3
Supervision of honors program	3.9	2.1
Research	33.0	45.8
Publication	28.2	40.6
Public service	29.1	35.4
Consultation (government, business)	1.9	5.2
Activity in professional societies	19.4	34.4
Student advising	55.3	43.8
Campus committee work	36.9	54.2
Length of service in rank	33.0	37.5
Competing job offers	1.9	2.1
Personal attributes	23.3	15.6

factor" by more than 11 percent, public service moved up by more than 6 percent, and personal attributes declined by more than 7 percent. In fact, in only five years, seven of the thirteen factors shifted in importance by 6 percent or more, a considerable movement.

Research, publication, and activity in professional societies, the traditional hallmarks of academic success, recorded sizable gains. In the words of a New York dean: "High visibility for our faculty is the name of the game today. If they do research, publish journal articles, and present papers at professional meetings, they will be in the public eye. And that's what our state legislators want. Since they control our budget dollars, we encourage our faculty to be active in their disciplines." There can be no doubt that research and publication are important criteria at many institutions where they are part of the stated mission. But there can also be no doubt that a revised rating game for professors is operating on the campuses of today's public colleges.

Study Highlights

1. The academic deans almost unanimously choose classroom performance as the most important index of overall faculty performance.

2. Private colleges give greater importance today than in the past to research, publication, public service, and activity in professional societies. Public colleges continue to venerate these factors.
3. Personal attributes, length of service in rank, and competing job offers are less widely cited today as important factors in promotion and tenure decisions.
4. Student advising is still widely cited by the private college deans as a major factor, although less frequently than in the past.
5. Liberal arts colleges report significant similarities and differences in their faculty evaluation practices.
6. On balance, greater importance is given today to a wider range of factors in an attempt to achieve reliability and scope in assessing overall faculty performance.

Evaluating Classroom Teaching: Findings

Almost all liberal arts colleges, private and public, designate classroom teaching effectiveness as the most important factor in faculty evaluation. That being the case, it is pertinent to inquire into the kind of information used to assess this effectiveness. Table 9 spells out the frequency with which deans of liberal arts colleges acknowledge a particular source of information as "always used" and compares this frequency with the 1978 study.

It is evident in Table 9 that some significant changes are transforming the ways in which liberal arts colleges assess sources of information in the evaluation of teaching performance. Of the fifteen sources, five changed by five percentage points or more, and, more significantly, they changed in the same direction. Each source is more widely used today. The trend over the past five years is evident. Information gathering is now more structured and systematic. A growing number of institutions are making concerted efforts to formalize and shore up their evaluative methods.

Which informational sources are most heavily relied on? The front-runner is still the evaluation by department chair and dean, with the chair's evaluation still dominant. But the gap between them widened from 3.4 percent to 6.3 percent in the five-year period.

Table 9. Frequency of Use of Sources of Information
Considered in Evaluating Teaching Performance
in Liberal Arts Colleges, 1978 and 1983.

Sources of Information	1978 (N = 680) Always Used %	1983 (N = 616) Always Used %
Systematic student ratings	54.8	67.5
Informal student opinions	15.2	11.5
Classroom visits	14.3	19.8
Colleagues' opinions	42.7	43.3
Scholarly research and publication	19.9	27.3
Student examination performance	2.7	3.6
Chair evaluation	80.3	81.3
Dean evaluation	76.9	75.0
Course syllabi and examinations	13.9	20.1
Long-term follow-up of students	2.2	3.4
Enrollment in elective courses	2.7	1.1
Alumni opinions	3.4	3.9
Committee evaluation	46.6	46.1
Grade distributions	2.1	4.5
Self-evaluation or report	36.6	41.9

Whether academic administrators make sound decisions in their evaluation of professors is a chronic question. Many believe it not only possible but also likely that administrators render sound decisions. In an analogy to clinical medicine, they point to experienced physicians who respond to subtle symptoms to arrive at a correct diagnosis. Yet they are often at a loss to explain the quantum leap from symptoms to diagnosis. Administrators have ready access, of course, to the circumstances of a professor's course load and student enrollment. But in the absence of personal classroom visits and/or examination of instructional materials, administrators are forced to fall back on secondary sources of information about a professor's competence as a teacher.

Quite probably, administrators continue to exercise their dominant role in the evaluation process because most professors perceive the administrative judgments as sound. It is more than possible that they *are* sound. Yet the question persists: Is the perception equal to the reality? How often not? How seriously?

The key question is, which sources of information do administrators rely on for their judgments? Very likely they rely, at least in part, on faculty committees. In many liberal arts colleges, faculty committees continue to play stellar roles in personnel decisions. In 1978 and again in 1983, more than 46 percent of the liberal arts colleges acknowledged faculty committees as "always used" as a source of evaluating teaching performance.

The question persists about faculty committees as well as chairpersons and deans. On what do they base their decisions? How sound is their information? Impressions of teaching competence are probably derived, at least in part, from the professors' research and publications. This source of information was "always used" by 19.9 percent of the deans in 1978 and climbed to 27.3 percent by 1983. Of course, justification for judging professors' classroom teaching by their publications is limited, or should be, to those publications offering insight into their teaching competency. But on the face of it, the number of textbooks, journal articles, and monographs offering such insight is extremely modest.

There is compelling evidence that both administrators and faculty committees rely on student ratings to help shape their own judgments of teaching competency. The use of written, formal student ratings jumped dramatically between 1978 and 1983. Today, perhaps for the first time, student ratings are "always used" in personnel decisions in more than two thirds of the liberal arts colleges. Students have an increasingly powerful voice in the assessment of their professors.

This shift of positions is also indicated in the t-tests of differences in mean scores of sources of information considered in evaluating teaching performance, as noted in Table 10. Analysis of Table 10 indicates significant differences at the 0.01 level of confidence between 1978 and 1983 mean scores of three sources of information—systematic student ratings, classroom visits, and course syllabi and examinations.

Classroom visits have not only expanded in the past five years, but their multiplication has also exacerbated the conflict over their value. "The only true way to know how a professor teaches is to see him in action," wrote a Massachusetts dean. "Classroom visitation is mandatory at our college." A contrary view was bluntly expressed by an Illinois dean: "Classroom visitation has no value."

Table 10. T-Tests of Differences in Mean Scores of Sources of
Information Considered in Evaluating Teaching Performance
in Liberal Arts Colleges, 1978 and 1983.

Sources of Information	1978 (N = 680) Mean Score	1983 (N = 616) Mean Score	t^a
Systematic student ratings	1.64	1.44	4.46[b]
Informal student opinions	2.31	2.41	– 2.03[c]
Classroom visits	2.67	2.43	4.60[b]
Colleagues' opinions	1.73	1.71	0.47
Scholarly research and publication	2.34	2.23	1.90
Student examination performance	3.08	3.03	1.20
Chair evaluation	1.27	1.26	0.15
Dean evaluation	1.32	1.36	– 1.18
Course syllabi and examinations	2.41	2.22	4.23[b]
Long-term follow-up of students	3.16	3.15	0.48
Enrollment in elective courses	3.04	3.12	– 2.02[c]
Alumni opinions	3.06	3.08	– 0.63
Committee evaluation	2.06	2.06	– 0.10
Grade distributions	3.12	3.07	0.90
Self-evaluation or report	2.08	1.96	2.02[c]

[a]The test used was a t-test for differences in independent proportions.
[b]Significant at 0.01 level of confidence.
[c]Significant at 0.05 level of confidence.

Teaching judgments are increasingly derived from an analysis of course syllabi and examinations. Central to this approach is whether such instructional materials are current, relevant, and suitable to the course. The growing use of handouts, reading lists, homework assignments, and student learning experiences, although not widespread, is consistent with today's trend to more structured information gathering.

Further analysis of Table 10 indicates significant differences at the 0.05 level of confidence between the 1978 and 1983 mean scores of three sources of information — informal student opinions, enrollment in elective courses, and self-evaluation or report. It comes as no surprise that reliance on informal student opinions has declined. These opinions were picked up in the past as scraps of information in chance encounters with students. Such random opinions have largely been replaced by systematic student ratings.

Self-evaluation has gained popularity as a useful tool in the assessment of teaching performance. Today, there is considerable recognition by liberal arts colleges that self-evaluation can and should play a significant role in a multisource evaluation process. Professors can and do produce not only insights into their own course and instructional objectives but also solid clues to their classroom teaching competency. Despite its popularity, however, self-evaluation as a tool in personnel decisions remains controversial. A supporter, an Oregon dean, wrote: "Self-evaluation is the keystone in our teaching appraisal system." An opponent, a New Jersey dean, argued: "Anyone being considered for tenure or promotion in rank is sure to provide a self-appraisal that portrays him as the greatest thing since sliced bread." Most opponents perceived self-evaluation as self-serving.

In 1973, the writer conducted a nationwide survey of sources of information "always used" in private liberal arts colleges in evaluating teaching performance. Table 11 shows the frequency found in that study and compares it to the 1978 and 1983

Table 11. Frequency of Use of Sources of Information
Considered in Evaluating Teaching Performance in
Private Liberal Arts Colleges, 1973, 1978, and 1983.

Sources of Information	1973 (N = 410) Always Used %	1978 (N = 567) Always Used %	1983 (N = 515) Always Used %
Systematic student ratings	29.1	53.1	66.6
Informal student opinions	17.8	16.9	12.8
Classroom visits	4.9	11.1	17.3
Colleagues' opinions	39.6	42.0	44.5
Scholarly research and publication	19.3	18.5	26.0
Student examination performance	3.7	3.2	3.5
Chair evaluation	85.3	79.9	81.9
Dean evaluation	85.3	77.4	76.9
Course syllabi and examinations	10.5	14.3	20.2
Long-term follow-up of students	2.2	2.6	3.7
Enrollment in elective courses	2.9	2.8	1.2
Alumni opinions	2.0	3.9	4.3
Committee evaluation	42.3	45.1	45.8
Grade distributions	2.4	2.5	5.0
Self-evaluation or report	19.8	36.3	42.5

studies. Certain major trends have emerged in the past ten years. First is a dramatic increase in the use of systematic student ratings and self-evaluation or report. Second is the growing reliance on classroom visits and course syllabi and examinations. (See Figure 1 for a graphic represention of these changes.)

Third, chair and dean evaluations are still the predominant sources of information, but with sharply diluted power. This power loss is seen in the closing gap between the first-place chair and dean and the second-place contender. In 1973, the second-place contender, committee evaluation, trailed by a distant 43.0 percent. By 1978, systematic student ratings had moved into second place, and the gap had narrowed to 26.8 percent. By 1983,

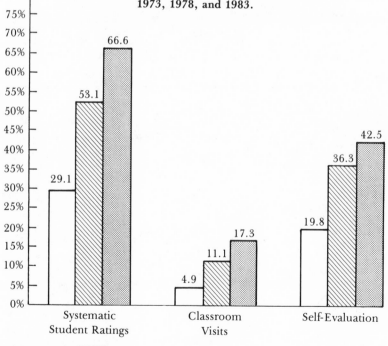

Figure 1. Percentage of Private Liberal Arts Colleges Using Systematic Student Ratings, Classroom Visits, and Self-Evaluation in Evaluating Teaching Performance, 1973, 1978, and 1983.

1973 (N = 410)
1978 (N = 567)
1983 (N = 515)

systematic student ratings, still in second place, had cut the margin to 15.3 percent.

Fourth, colleagues' opinions and committee evaluation seem firmly entrenched as heavyweight sources of information in evaluating teaching performance.

Fifth, consistently at the bottom of the list in each of the three surveys are long-term follow-up of students, enrollments in elective courses, alumni opinions, grade distribution, and student examination performance.

To summarize, on the basis of the three studies, there is no doubt that private liberal arts colleges in the past decade have been busy dismantling and reconstructing some of their procedures in the faculty evaluation system. This reshaping is also indicated in the t-tests of differences in mean scores of sources of information considered in appraising teaching performance (Table 12).

A data analysis indicates significant differences at the 0.01

Table 12. T-Tests of Differences in Mean Scores of Sources of Information Considered in Evaluating Faculty Teaching Performance in Private Liberal Arts Colleges, 1973 and 1983.

Sources of Information	1973 (N = 410) Mean Score	1983 (N = 515) Mean Score	t^a
Systematic student ratings	2.20	1.45	13.57^b
Informal student opinions	2.04	2.35	-6.40^b
Classroom visits	2.98	2.48	8.99^b
Colleagues' opinions	1.76	1.69	1.42
Scholarly research and publication	2.30	2.28	0.31
Student examination performance	2.95	3.03	-1.47
Chair evaluation	1.22	1.26	-0.87
Dean evaluation	1.19	1.33	-3.40^b
Course syllabi and examinations	2.56	2.21	6.41^b
Long-term follow-up of students	3.13	3.13	-0.08
Enrollment in elective courses	2.79	3.09	-6.07^b
Alumni opinions	3.09	3.05	0.97
Committee evaluation	2.17	2.06	1.38
Grade distributions	3.05	3.04	0.23
Self-evaluation or report	2.58	1.95	9.24^b

[a]The test used was a t-test for differences in independent proportions.
[b]Significant at 0.01 level of confidence.

level of confidence between 1973 and 1983 mean scores of seven sources of information — systematic student ratings, informal student opinions, classroom visits, dean evaluation, course syllabi and examinations, enrollment in elective courses, and self-evaluation. Also indicated is a change in the number of sources of information rated toward the low end. In the 1973 study, only three sources — colleagues' opinions, chair evaluation, and dean evaluation — earned a mean score rating of less than 2.00. But in the 1983 study, five sources — the same three plus systematic student ratings and self-evaluation — earned the same low rating. This increase in the number of sources with low mean scores suggests that private colleges increasingly are considering a wider range of sources in evaluating faculty performance in the classroom.

These statistical trends were given voice by many deans. An Ohio dean wrote: "Evaluation of teaching is different now. We used to make decisions on the basis of soft information and hunch. Today, we systematically obtain data from many sources and weigh it all carefully before reaching judgments." A Texas dean wrote: "Our rule of thumb is, the more sources the better." From a Florida dean: "We've devoted hundreds of hours and thousands of dollars to create a more effective system to appraise teaching. Today, our approach is more systematic and structured. We rely on many data sources and insist on written forms to gather information."

Private liberal arts colleges are not alone in modifying their evaluation approaches. Public colleges, also, have reconstructed their approaches. Base data for public colleges in 1973 are, unfortunately, unavailable, but a comparison of the 1978 and 1983 surveys points to numerous changes. Table 13 summarizes the public college deans' consideration in evaluating faculty classroom performance. Of the fifteen sources of information listed for the 1978 and 1983 surveys, six moved up or down by 5 percent or more — systematic student ratings, colleagues' opinions, scholarly research and publication, dean evaluation, course syllabi and examinations, and committee evaluation.

Cited most frequently as "always used" in the 1983 survey are evaluations by department chair and dean (79.2 percent and

Table 13. Frequency of Use of Sources of Information
Considered in Evaluating Teaching Performance
in Public Liberal Arts Colleges, 1978 and 1983.

Sources of Information	1978 (N = 103) Always Used %	1983 (N = 96) Always Used %
Systematic student ratings	64.1	71.9
Informal student opinions	5.8	4.2
Classroom visits	32.0	34.4
Colleagues' opinions	46.6	38.5
Scholarly research and publication	27.2	34.4
Student examination performance	8.7	4.2
Chair evaluation	82.5	79.2
Dean evaluation	73.8	65.6
Course syllabi and examinations	11.7	20.8
Long-term follow-up of students	0.0	2.1
Enrollment in elective courses	1.9	1.0
Alumni opinions	1.0	2.1
Committee evaluation	54.4	47.9
Grade distributions	0.0	2.1
Self-evaluation or report	37.9	39.6

65.6 percent, respectively). Although the importance of administrative judgments in faculty evaluation remains strong, the past five years have witnessed a slippage for the department chair (3.3 percent) and for the dean (8.2 percent). Clearly, administrators have lost some of their monarchical power. In fact, deans have now been surpassed by systematic student ratings as the second most widely used source of information in evaluating teaching performance.

Scholarly research and publication has gained importance as a measure of teaching competency, although on the face of it the relationship between the two seems remote. It is difficult to see how good research translates into good classroom teaching. Given special circumstances, it is conceivable that professors' enthusiasm and seminal thinking about their scholarly research and publication ignite their students. But those are special cases, indeed. It is far more likely that the positive values of scholarly research and publication are presumptively grafted onto classroom teaching. Very few monographs, journal articles, books, and book reviews provide trustworthy clues to teaching ability.

In both the 1978 and 1983 studies, informal student opinion, long-term follow-up of students, enrollment in elective courses, alumni opinions, and grade distributions were at the bottom of the list as important sources of information.

Table 14 shows the distribution of "always used" and "never used" responses by private and public college deans to a range of information sources. Several vital similarities and differences in the evaluative thinking of private and public college deans are exhibited. Both deans give top marks to chair and dean evaluations of classroom teaching, but at public colleges, the chair's evaluation is given considerably more weight than the dean's.

The deans at private colleges depend on colleagues' opinions and self-evaluation much more than do public college deans, who are more dependent on systematic student ratings, classroom visits, scholarly research and publication, and committee evaluation. Scant attention is paid at both colleges to student examination performance, long-term follow-up of students,

Table 14. Frequency of Use of Sources of Information
Considered in Evaluating Teaching Performance in
Liberal Arts Colleges, 1983.

Sources of Information	Private Colleges (N = 515)		Public Colleges (N = 96)	
	Always Used %	Never Used %	Always Used %	Never Used %
Systematic student ratings	66.6	1.9	71.9	1.0
Informal student opinions	12.8	5.8	4.2	16.7
Classroom visits	17.3	9.7	34.4	10.4
Colleagues' opinions	44.5	0.8	38.5	2.1
Scholarly research and publication	26.0	9.5	34.4	4.2
Student examination performance	3.5	26.8	4.2	30.2
Chair evaluation	81.9	2.5	79.2	2.1
Dean evaluation	76.9	2.3	65.6	3.1
Course syllabi and examinations	20.2	5.0	20.8	4.2
Long-term follow-up of students	3.7	30.9	2.1	37.5
Enrollment in elective courses	1.2	30.3	1.0	40.6
Alumni opinions	4.3	25.4	2.1	38.5
Committee evaluation	45.8	17.5	47.9	14.6
Grade distributions	5.0	29.3	2.1	39.6
Self-evaluation or report	42.5	8.7	39.6	9.4

enrollment in elective courses, alumni opinions, and grade distribution.

Surprisingly, private and public colleges report considerable internal divergence in some practices. For example, committee evaluation is "always used" by almost 46 percent of the private and 48 percent of the public colleges, but almost 18 percent of one and 15 percent of the other "never used" committee evaluation. Similarly, classroom visits were "always used" by about 17 percent of the private and 34 percent of the public colleges, but about 10 percent of both institutions "never used" classroom visits.

However, despite the divergence in some practices, there is considerable uniformity in the approaches of private and public colleges to teaching evaluations. For example, both report systematic student ratings "always used" by more than 66 percent and "never used" by fewer than 2 percent. Again, chair and dean evaluations are "always used" by a hefty majority of both institutions, whereas only a handful "never used" them.

Table 15 shows the percentage of institutions using rating forms (whether completed by students, colleagues, or administrators) and the percentage conducting research on the instruments used. Almost 70 percent of the colleges used rating forms of one kind or another in 1983, a climb of seven percentage points since 1978. What is still disheartening, however, is the persistent minimal research by the institutions on the validity of the forms used to judge their faculty. Only 10 percent of the colleges engaged in such research in 1978, and this figure barely moved in the next five years. Without a supportive base of research, an evaluative source of information risks being dropped and replaced by a more

Table 15. Frequency of Use and Research on Rating Forms
to Evaluate Faculty Teaching Performance
in Liberal Arts Colleges, 1978 and 1983.

	1978 (N = 680)	1983 (N = 616)
Do you use special rating forms?	62.8	69.8
Has your institution conducted research on the validity of these rating forms?	10.0	11.2

fashionable evaluative tool. Is it possible that the lack of interest in research reflects an underlying distrust of the rating forms by many faculty members and even administrators?

Study Highlights

1. The department chair and dean are still the predominant information sources on teaching performance.
2. Impressions of teaching performance based on a professor's research and publication record are more widely used today.
3. The evidence is compelling that administrators rely on student ratings, whose use has jumped dramatically, to help shape their own judgments of teaching competency.
4. Classroom visits, course syllabi and examinations, and faculty self-evaluation have gained popularity as tools in the assessment of classroom teaching performance.
5. Faculty committees continue to play stellar roles in evaluating teaching performance.
6. Reliance on informal student opinions, enrollment in elective courses, and alumni opinions is losing importance.
7. Liberal arts colleges, in altering their appraisal practices, are today obtaining data from systematic and public sources and cover a broader range.

Evaluating Scholarship/Research: Findings

Table 16 shows the frequency with which deans "always used" a source of information in evaluating scholarship/research in 1983 and compares this frequency with the 1978 study. Even a cursory examination of Table 16 shows the stepped-up reliance in the past five years on all the listed sources of information, with one exception. Citations in published materials declined in the face of an average percentage jump of nearly five points for every other source of information. This consistently greater reliance on all but one of the listed sources suggests the need and desire of deans for a wider base from which to judge the professor's scholarship/ research performance. This was frequently articulated by the deans. A California dean wrote: "We are making a determined effort to evaluate scholarship/research, and we look hard at data

Table 16. Frequency of Use of Information Considered in
Evaluating Scholarship/Research Performance in
Liberal Arts Colleges, 1978 and 1983.

Types of Information	1978 (N = 680) Always Used %	1983 (N = 616) Always Used %
Publication in all professional journals	46.0	54.1
Articles in quality journals	44.5	51.8
Unpublished papers or reports	13.7	17.0
Papers at professional meetings	41.8	44.8
Citations in published materials	14.0	13.5
Books as sole or senior author	53.1	58.1
Books as junior author or editor	46.7	54.7
Monographs or chapters in books	47.8	52.0
Quality of Research and Publication as Judged by:		
Peers at the institution	42.5	46.3
Peers at other institutions	11.5	14.1
Department chair	47.9	50.8
Academic dean	40.4	44.8
Self-evaluation	19.7	26.9
Grants or funding received	22.8	29.1
Referee or editor of professional journal	19.4	25.6
Honors or awards from profession	38.5	46.9

from many sources." A Texas dean wrote: "Now we consider
books, articles, monographs, papers at conferences, even citations
in the literature in judging research and publication."

Liberal arts colleges continue to give highest marks to
books written by a professor as the sole or senior author. But
nearly as important are books written as junior author, publication in professional journals, monographs and chapters in books,
and articles in quality journals.

Of the eight types of information listed in the two surveys,
1978 and 1983, and cited as "always used," four moved up by 5
percent or more and two by about 8 percent.

On the quality of research/publication, each of the eight
sources of information reported "always used" gained about 5 per-

cent in the five years. Most widely cited as judges of quality were department chair, peers at the institution, and honors or awards from the profession. These changes in the way in which scholarship/research was evaluated in 1978 and 1983 are seen in the t-tests of differences in mean scores of types of information considered (Table 17).

Data analysis in Table 17 indicates significant differences at the 0.01 level of confidence between the mean scores of three types of information in the 1978 and 1983 surveys — publication in all professional journals, articles in quality journals, and books

Table 17. T-Tests of Differences in Mean Scores of Information Considered in Evaluating Scholarship/Research Performance in Liberal Arts Colleges, 1978 and 1983.

Types of Information	1978 (N = 680) Mean Score	1983 (N = 616) Mean Score	t^a
Publication in all professional journals	1.79	1.63	3.16[b]
Articles in quality journals	1.84	1.69	2.67[b]
Unpublished papers or reports	2.47	2.39	1.53
Papers at professional meetings	1.79	1.69	1.92
Citations in published materials	2.68	2.61	1.16
Books as sole or senior author	1.76	1.63	2.30[c]
Books as junior author or editor	1.86	1.67	3.13[b]
Monographs or chapters in books	1.80	1.68	2.18[c]
Total Mean	2.00	1.87	
Quality of Research and Publication as Judged by:			
Peers at the institution	1.93	1.86	1.10
Peers at other institutions	2.84	2.72	2.09[c]
Department chair	1.79	1.73	1.10
Academic dean	1.91	1.86	0.99
Self-evaluation	2.51	2.33	2.93[b]
Grants or funding received	2.37	2.18	2.98[b]
Referee or editor of professional journal	2.69	2.39	4.63[b]
Honors or awards from profession	1.94	1.79	2.72[b]
Total Mean	2.25	2.11	

[a]The test was a t-test for differences in independent proportions.
[b]Significant at 0.01 level of confidence.
[c]Significant at 0.05 level of confidence.

as junior author or editor. Significant differences at the 0.05 level are found between the mean scores of two types of information — books as sole or senior author and monographs or chapters in books. Changes of similar magnitude turn up in judging the quality of research and publication. Statistically significant differences between the mean scores of the two surveys were found for five items. Significant at the 0.01 level were self-evaluation, grants or funding received, referee or editor of professional journal, and honors or awards from the profession. One item, peers at other institutions, was significant at the 0.05 level. Every item whose change was significant statistically changed in the same direction and achieved a lower mean score in 1983 than in 1978. This suggests that liberal arts colleges are more attentive

Table 18. Frequency of Use of Information Considered in
Evaluating Scholarship/Research Performance in
Private Liberal Arts Colleges, 1978 and 1983.

Types of Information	1978 (N = 567) Always Used %	1983 (N = 515) Always Used %
Publication in all professional journals	45.0	52.8
Articles in quality journals	42.5	49.1
Unpublished papers or reports	14.3	16.7
Papers at professional meetings	39.9	42.5
Citations in published materials	13.8	12.6
Books as sole or senior author	50.1	56.3
Books as junior author or editor	44.6	52.6
Monographs or chapters in books	45.5	49.9
Quality of Research and Publication as Judged by:		
Peers at the institution	42.3	45.4
Peers at other institutions	11.3	14.2
Department chair	47.4	50.7
Academic dean	40.0	44.7
Self-evaluation	19.0	26.4
Grants or funding received	21.9	27.6
Referee or editor of professional journal	16.9	23.7
Honors or awards from profession	36.9	44.7

to more types of information and to the judges of that information in the evaluation of a professor's scholarship/research.

Table 18 compares types of information "always used" by academic deans in private colleges in evaluating faculty scholarship/ research in 1978 and 1983. It is quickly apparent that the information-gathering process has expanded, and today, virtually every available type of information is employed, and by greater numbers of deans. But the most popular sources among the deans are books as sole or senior author, publication in all professional journals, and books as junior author or editor. Only one replacement has been made among the three front-runners since 1978: monographs or chapters in books has been nosed out by books as junior author or editor.

In both studies, of least interest to the deans as sources were citations in published materials and unpublished papers or reports, although a surprising 16.7 percent of the deans "always used" the latter by 1983. In judging the quality of the research and publication, private colleges in both studies looked first to the department chair and then to faculty peers, the academic dean, and honors or awards from profession. Worthy of note is that honors or awards from profession recorded the largest jump — almost 8 percent — in the past five years.

Table 19 indicates which types of information were "always used" by public liberal arts colleges in 1983 in appraising scholarship/ research as compared to 1978. The most striking change, perhaps, is that today, five different types of information (against two in 1978) are reported "always used" by 60 percent or more of the public college deans. This sizable increase suggests strenuous efforts by the public colleges to parade the results of their faculty's scholarship/research so as to convince state legislators of the wisdom of public funding. This view receives support in comments by some deans. An Arizona dean wrote: "Our public board of overseers insists on tangible proof that the faculty is engaged in high-level research. Since the board controls the budget, we push the faculty to produce publication." A Michigan dean put it bluntly: "This college will perish if the faculty does not publish."

Books as sole or senior author was the type of information cited most frequently in both surveys. But the gap between first

Table 19. Frequency of Use of Information Considered in
Evaluating Scholarship/Research Performance in
Public Liberal Arts Colleges, 1978 and 1983.

Types of Information	1978 (N = 103) Always Used %	1983 (N = 96) Always Used %
Publication in all professional journals	51.5	61.5
Articles in quality journals	55.3	67.7
Unpublished papers or reports	10.7	18.8
Papers at professional meetings	52.4	58.3
Citations in published materials	15.5	17.7
Books as sole or senior author	69.9	68.8
Books as junior author or editor	58.3	67.7
Monographs or chapters in books	60.2	64.6
Quality of Research and Publication as Judged by:		
Peers at the institution	43.7	53.1
Peers at other institutions	12.6	13.5
Department chair	50.5	53.1
Academic dean	42.7	46.9
Self-evaluation	23.3	31.3
Grants or funding received	28.2	38.5
Referee or editor of professional journal	33.0	37.5
Honors or awards from profession	47.6	61.5

and second place diminished from almost 10 percent in 1978 to about 1 percent in 1983. In fact, bunched together and trailing the leader by only a few percent, a number of types of information contended in importance. Of the eight types of information, six increased by 4 percent or more by 1983 — publication in all professional journals, articles in quality journals, unpublished papers or reports, papers at professional meetings, books as junior author or editor, and monographs or chapters in books. And three of those types of information jumped by more than 9 percent — publication in all professional journals, articles in quality journals, and books as junior author or editor.

As for judging the quality of research and publication, honors or awards from profession shot into first place, indicating the pressing need of public colleges for public recognition. Almost 62 percent of the deans "always used" honors or awards from profession as a quality yardstick in 1983, a leap of almost 14 percent in five years. Other judges of importance were the department chair and the professor's peers at the institution, the latter gaining almost 10 percent. Actually, all eight categories of quality assessment recorded gains from 1978 to 1983, with seven of the eight cited as "always used" by more than 31 percent to almost 62 percent of the deans. Thus, quality of research and publication is today receiving more attention by more deans from more indices.

Table 20 shows which types of information were "always used" by private and public college deans in evaluating a profes-

Table 20. Frequency of Use of Information Considered in Evaluating Scholarship/Research Performance in Liberal Arts Colleges, 1983.

Types of Information	Private Colleges (N = 515) Always Used %	Public Colleges (N = 96) Always Used %
Publication in all professional journals	52.8	61.5
Articles in quality journals	49.1	67.7
Unpublished papers or reports	16.7	18.8
Papers at professional meetings	42.5	58.3
Citations in published materials	12.6	17.7
Books as sole or senior author	56.3	68.8
Books as junior author or editor	52.6	67.7
Monographs or chapters in books	49.9	64.6
Quality of Research and Publication as Judged by:		
Peers at the institution	45.4	53.1
Peers at other institutions	14.2	13.5
Department chair	50.7	53.1
Academic dean	44.7	46.9
Self-evaluation	26.4	31.3
Grants or funding received	27.6	38.5
Referee or editor of professional journal	23.7	37.5
Honors or awards from profession	44.7	61.5

sor's scholarship/research. One point stands out: In every case, the public college deans place higher store on the value of each type of information than do the private college deans. Virtually the same is true in the matter of assessing the quality of the professor's research and publication. (See Figure 2 for a graphic representation of this point.)

For most types of information, the gap between private and public college deans ranges from more than 10 percent to almost 20 percent. For example, 61 percent or more of the public college deans "always used" publication in all professional journals, articles in quality journals, books as sole or senior author, books as

Figure 2. Percentage of Liberal Arts Colleges Using Articles in Quality Journals, Papers at Professional Meetings, and Honors and Awards from Profession in Evaluating Faculty Scholarship/Research Performance, 1983.

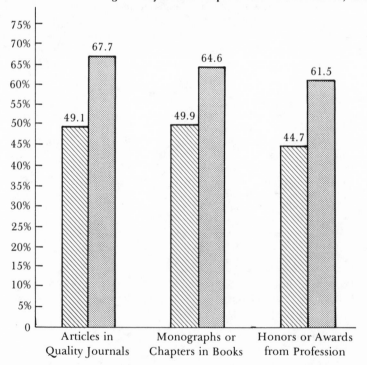

Private Colleges (N = 515)
Public Colleges (N = 96)

junior author or editor, and monographs or chapters in books in evaluating a professor's scholarship/research. But none of these indices turned up higher than 56.3 percent for the private college deans.

Also, on the matter of presenting papers at professional meetings, about 58 percent of the public college deans "always used" this category, whereas only about 42 percent of the private college deans accorded it such importance. Some of the deans wrote about their views. A private college dean said: "Papers at professional meetings are not given much weight. They are not in the same league with publications." A public college dean wrote: "We need to stay in the public eye. Publication is one way to do it, and papers at professional meetings is another." Similarly, the private colleges look first to their department chair in judging the quality of research and publication, whereas the public colleges give the nod to honors or awards from profession.

All of this suggests the public colleges' greater sensitivity to — and dependency on — state legislatures and other public forces. This would help explain their prolific use of grants or funding received, referee or editor of professional journal, and honors or awards from profession in measuring the quality of research/ publication. This difference between private and public liberal arts colleges is expressed in t-tests of differences in mean scores of types of information considered in evaluating scholarship/ research (see Table 21).

An analysis of Table 21 indicates significant differences at the 0.01 level between the mean scores of six types of information handled in the private and public colleges — articles in quality journals, papers at professional meetings, citations in published materials, books as sole or senior author, books as junior author or editor, and monographs or chapters in books. The total mean score for primate colleges is 1.92, for higher than the 1.66 mean score for private colleges is 1.92, far higher than the 1.66 mean score for public colleges. This suggests that private colleges are important than research/scholarship. Significant differences at the 0.01 level were also found between the mean scores of three items used in judging the quality of scholarship/research — grants or funding received, referee or editor of professional journal, and

Table 21. T-Tests of Differences in Mean Scores of Types of
Information Considered in Evaluating Scholarship/Research
Performance in Private and Public Liberal Arts Colleges,
1983.

Types of Information	Private Colleges (N = 515) Mean Score	Public Colleges (N = 96) Mean Score	t^a
Publication in all professional journals	1.65	1.50	1.62
Articles in quality journals	1.74	1.42	3.12[b]
Unpublished papers or reports	2.41	2.32	0.88
Papers at professional meetings	1.74	1.46	3.15[b]
Citations in published materials	2.66	2.36	2.91[b]
Books as sole or senior author	1.68	1.36	2.99[b]
Books as junior author or editor	1.72	1.40	3.07[b]
Monographs or chapters in books	1.72	1.45	2.72[b]
Total Mean	1.92	1.66	
Quality of Research and Publication as Judged by:			
Peers at the institution	1.88	1.74	1.14
Peers at other institutions	2.72	2.71	0.16
Department chair	1.75	1.63	1.09
Academic dean	1.87	1.80	0.59
Self-evaluation	2.35	2.25	0.79
Grants or funding received	2.24	1.86	3.29[b]
Referee or editor of professional journal	2.46	2.05	3.26[b]
Honors or awards from profession	1.85	1.46	3.64[b]
Total Mean	2.14	1.94	

[a]The test was a t-test for differences in independent proportions.
[b]Significant at 0.01 level of confidence.

honors or awards from profession. The fact that public colleges
came in with a lower total mean score points to a more catholic
appraisal of the quality of professorial research and publication.

Table 22 shows the types of information "always used" or
"never used" by academic deans in evaluating scholarship/research.
As previously observed, public colleges depend on more types of
information and on more judges in evaluating quality. Almost
invariably, the public college deans "always used" items with

Table 22. Frequency of Use of Information Considered in
Evaluating Scholarship/Research Performance in
Liberal Arts Colleges, 1983.

	Private Colleges (N = 515)		Public Colleges (N = 96)	
	Always Used %	Never Used %	Always Used %	Never Used %
Types of Information				
Publication in all professional journals	52.8	4.7	61.5	3.1
Articles in quality journals	49.1	5.0	67.7	4.2
Unpublished papers or reports	16.7	10.3	18.8	6.3
Papers at professional meetings	42.5	3.7	58.3	1.0
Citations in published materials	12.6	17.3	17.7	6.7
Books as sole or senior author	56.3	6.2	68.8	2.1
Books as junior author or editor	52.6	6.0	67.7	2.1
Monographs or chapters in books	49.9	5.0	64.6	3.1
Quality of Research and Publication as Judged by:				
Peers at the institution	45.4	9.5	53.1	7.1
Peers at other institutions	14.2	22.5	13.5	17.7
Department chair	50.7	8.0	53.1	6.3
Academic dean	44.7	8.0	46.9	7.3
Self-evaluation	26.4	17.5	31.3	13.5
Grants or funding received	27.6	13.4	38.5	7.3
Referee or editor of professional journal	23.7	19.6	37.5	11.5
Honors or awards from profession	44.7	7.2	61.5	2.1

greater frequency than did private college deans. But for both
private and public colleges, a surprisingly wide swing in response
is frequently reported. For example, 12.6 percent of the private
colleges "always used" citations in published materials, whereas
17.3 percent "never used" them. Again, 14.2 percent of the private
colleges "always used" peers at other institutions to judge the quality of research/publication, but 22.5 percent "never used" them.
And 31.3 percent of the public college deans "always used" self-
evaluation, whereas 13.5 percent "never used" it. It is clear that
neither private nor public liberal arts colleges apply uniform standards in the assessment of faculty scholarship/research.

Study Highlights

1. Academic deans consistently report greater reliance on more sources of information to judge a professor's scholarship/research performance.
2. Liberal arts colleges continue to give highest marks to books written by a professor as th* sole or senior author. Almost as important are books writte.1 as junior author, publication in professional journals, monographs and chapters in books, and articles in quality journals.
3. Honors or awards from profession has gained considerable importance and is now cited as a quality yardstick by nearly 50 percent of the liberal arts colleges.
4. The department chair, academic dean, and peers at the institution are most frequently cited as judges of quality.
5. Self-evaluation and grants or funding are more important today, but not widely used.
6. All ten items whose change between 1978 and 1983 is statistically significant changed in the same direction: all are more frequently used today.

Evaluating College Service: Findings

For generations, college service has been respected as the third benchmark, after teaching and research/publication, in evaluating overall faculty performance. Table 23 shows how often deans "always used" each of the nine factors in evaluating a professor's college service in 1983 and compares this frequency with the 1978 study. The situation in the past five years has remained largely unchanged. In fact, of the nine factors, only two—willingness to teach undesirable courses and participation in campus symposia—changed by 4 percent or more. The other seven factors, aside from minor changes, were almost uniformly the same in 1983 as they were in 1978. This is reflected in the average score for all factors, which in both studies was 38.3 percent.

Service on collegewide committees and academic advising stand out in 1983, as they did in 1978, as "always used" by more deans than any other factor. Service on collegewide committees is cited today by almost 83 percent of the deans (a gain of 3 percent)

Table 23. Frequency of Use of Factors Considered in
Evaluating College Service Performance in
Liberal Arts Colleges, 1978 and 1983.

Factors	1978 (N = 680) Always Used %	1983 (N = 616) Always Used %
Service on department committee	45.1	47.4
Service on collegewide committee	79.7	82.8
Academic advising	79.7	76.8
Nonacademic student counseling	22.8	19.0
Willingness to teach undesirable courses	20.1	15.9
Adviser to student organizations	21.3	20.6
Service as student recruiter	11.6	12.0
Departmental administrative duties	43.9	45.1
Participation in campus symposia	20.9	25.5

and academic advising by almost 77 percent (a loss of 3 percent). Willingness to teach undesirable courses and service as student recruiter remain in the cellar, with about one dean in five acknowledging he "always used" them in evaluations. Service on department committee and departmental administrative duties continue to weigh in as important considerations, and each has picked up a bit more importance in the five years. Although not a major factor, participation in campus symposia recorded the largest gain, almost 5 percent, and today is "always used" by about one quarter of the deans.

The stability of these figures over five years is revealed in Table 24, which shows t-tests of differences in the mean scores of the factors. There is significant difference at the 0.05 level between the 1978 and 1983 mean scores of only one factor, participation in campus symposia. The almost identical mean scores suggest that, despite financial distress in recent years, no substantial change has been wrought in the liberal arts colleges' evaluation practices relating to college service. Table 25 shows how private college deans viewed the nine factors in evaluating college service in 1978 and 1983. These factors fall into four categories of decreasing importance. First, and most important, are service on collegewide

Table 24. T-Tests of Differences in Mean Scores of Factors
Considered in Evaluating College Service Performance in
Liberal Arts Colleges, 1978 and 1983.

Factors	1978 (N = 680) Mean Score	1983 (N = 616) Mean Score	t^a
Service on department committee	1.54	1.54	-0.25
Service on collegewide committee	1.20	1.16	1.54
Academic advising	1.20	1.24	-1.91
Nonacademic student counseling	1.92	1.98	-1.81
Willingness to teach undesirable courses	2.04	2.09	-1.31
Adviser to student organizations	1.89	1.89	-0.04
Service as student recruiter	2.16	2.11	1.39
Departmental administrative duties	1.62	1.59	0.55
Participation in campus symposia	1.93	1.85	2.00^b
Total mean	1.75	1.74	

[a]The test used was a t-test for differences in independent proportions.
[b]Significant at 0.05 level of confidence.

committee and academic advising, which about 81 percent of the private college deans "always used" in evaluations. Second are service on department committee and departmental administrative duties, each "always used" by about 45 percent of the deans. Third are nonacademic student counseling, adviser to student organizations, and participation in campus symposia, cited by about 23 percent. Fourth, and least important, are willingness to teach undesirable courses and service as student recruiter, each "always used" by about 15 percent of the deans. Despite the ebb and flow by a few percent from 1978 to 1983, no factor left its category of importance.

Table 26 shows how often public college deans "always used" each of the nine factors in evaluating college service and compares this frequency with the 1978 study. Service on collegewide committee is far ahead of any other factor "always used" by public college deans and clearly plays the star role in the evaluation of college service. It is considered so important that it even picked up an additional 8 percent in the last five years, climbing from 76.7 percent to 84.4 percent. In second place is academic advising, which is "always used" by almost 60 percent of the deans, a slippage of more than 6 percent from 1978. In fact, academic

Table 25. Frequency of Use of Factors Considered in
Evaluating College Service Performance in
Private Liberal Arts Colleges, 1978 and 1983.

Factors	1978 (N = 567) Always Used %	1983 (N = 515) Always Used %
Service on department committee	43.4	46.2
Service on collegewide committee	80.2	82.9
Academic advising	82.2	80.2
Nonacademic student counseling	25.0	21.2
Willingness to teach undesirable courses	20.6	16.9
Adviser to student organizations	21.9	21.2
Service as student recruiter	11.8	12.8
Departmental administrative duties	44.4	45.6
Participation in campus symposia	22.0	25.0

advising is in danger of losing second place to service on department committee, which gained slightly.

The devaluation of academic advising is perhaps explained by the urgent need of public colleges for public approbation of their faculties. Academic advising is ordinarily a private discussion between professor and student behind a closed door, a process that attracts little public attention, much less acclaim. Partic-

Table 26. Frequency of Use of Factors Considered in
Evaluating College Service Performance in
Public Liberal Arts Colleges, 1978 and 1983.

Factors	1978 (N = 103) Always Used %	1983 (N = 96) Always Used %
Service on department committee	54.4	55.2
Service on collegewide committee	76.7	84.4
Academic advising	66.0	59.4
Nonacademic student counseling	10.7	8.3
Willingness to teach undesirable courses	17.5	11.5
Adviser to student organizations	18.4	18.8
Service as student recruiter	10.7	7.3
Departmental administrative duties	40.8	43.8
Participation in campus symposia	14.6	29.2

ipation in campus symposia is "always used" by almost 30 percent of the deans, a dramatic jump of almost 15 percent in five years, and probably for the same reason. Campus symposia on hot topics often attract a packed house and considerable coverage in the press. It should come as no surprise, therefore, that behind-the-scenes activities such as nonacademic student counseling and service as student recruiter are "always used" by fewer than 10 percent of the deans.

Table 27 shows how often private college deans "always used" factors to appraise college service and compares this frequency with that of public college deans. Public and private colleges are agreed that service on collegewide committees is the most important service a professor can proffer. About 83 percent of the private colleges and 84 percent of the public colleges "always used" this factor in evaluations. Such is not the case with academic advising, the second-place factor for both institutions but accorded much greater recognition at private colleges (80.2 percent) than at public colleges (59.4 percent). In the words of a private college dean: "We give skill as an academic adviser enormous weight in tenure and promotion decisions." In contrast, a public college dean wrote: "Academic advising has its place, but it is not nearly so critical in personnel decisions as service on collegewide committees."

**Table 27. Frequency of Use of Factors Considered in
Evaluating College Service Performance in
Liberal Arts Colleges, 1983.**

Factors	Private Colleges (N = 515) Always Used %	Public Colleges (N = 96) Always Used %
Service on department committee	46.2	55.2
Service on collegewide committee	82.9	84.4
Academic advising	80.2	59.4
Nonacademic student counseling	21.2	8.3
Willingness to teach undesirable courses	16.9	11.5
Adviser to student organizations	21.2	18.8
Service as student recruiter	12.8	7.3
Departmental administrative duties	45.6	43.8
Participation in campus symposia	25.0	29.2

Consistent with their high regard for academic advising, private college deans in much greater numbers than public college deans "always used" nonacademic student counseling and service as student recruiter in evaluating college service. Both private and public colleges checked in with about 45 percent for departmental administrative duties.

This agreement and disagreement in perception are indicated in the t-tests of differences in mean scores of factors considered in evaluating college service (see Table 28). Data analysis of Table 28 indicates significant differences at the 0.01 level between the mean scores of four factors — academic advising, nonacademic student counseling, willingness to teach undesirable courses, and service as student recruiter. In every instance, the mean score was lower for private colleges, indicating the greater importance attached to those factors by private colleges than by public colleges.

The mean score for service on collegewide committee is exceptionally low for both colleges, indicating the critical importance of that factor to both. The four factors with the lowest mean scores, similar for both colleges, are departmental administrative duties, academic advising, service on collegewide committee, and service on department committee.

Table 28. T-Tests of Differences in Mean Scores of Factors Considered in Evaluating College Service Performance in Liberal Arts Colleges, 1983.

Factors	Private Colleges (N = 515) Mean Score	Public Colleges (N = 96) Mean Score	t^a
Service on department committee	1.56	1.45	1.66
Service on collegewide committee	1.17	1.15	0.42
Academic advising	1.20	1.46	-4.98^b
Nonacademic student counseling	1.93	2.29	-5.21^b
Willingness to teach undesirable courses	2.07	2.22	-1.99^b
Adviser to student organizations	1.88	1.93	-0.87
Service as student recruiter	2.08	2.26	-2.62^b
Departmental administrative duties	1.59	1.61	-0.34
Participation in campus symposia	1.86	1.80	0.80

[a]The test was a t-test for differences in independent proportions.
[b]Significant at 0.01 level of confidence.

Table 29 shows the factors that are considered "major" or "not a factor" by deans in the evaluation of college service. It indicates that, while service on collegewide committee is the predominant factor in service evaluations in both private and public colleges, other factors receive deferential treatment. These are academic advising, service on department committee, and departmental administrative duties. Lightweight considerations include willingness to teach undesirable courses and service as student recruiter. Aside from this general overlapping, however, a wide chasm separates private and public colleges. While private colleges stress academic advising, nonacademic student counseling, and service as student recruiter, public colleges look to service on department committee and participation in campus symposia.

A chasm also separates private colleges from each other and public colleges from each other. For example, although 12.8 percent of the private college deans consider service as student recruiter a "major factor," 20 percent of them consider it "not a factor." And although 21.2 percent of them refer to nonacademic student counseling as a "major factor," to 14.2 percent it is "not a factor." Similarly, although 18.8 percent of the public college deans consider

Table 29. Relative Weight Assigned to Factors Considered in
Evaluating College Service Performance in
Liberal Arts Colleges, 1983.

Factors	Private Colleges (N = 515)		Public Colleges (N = 96)	
	Major Factor %	Not a Factor %	Major Factor %	Not a Factor %
Service on department committee	46.2	4.3	55.2	1.0
Service on collegewide committee	82.9	0.6	84.4	0.0
Academic advising	80.2	1.2	59.4	6.3
Nonacademic student counseling	21.2	14.2	8.3	35.4
Willingness to teach undesirable courses	16.9	23.3	11.5	31.3
Adviser to student organizations	21.2	9.5	18.8	12.5
Service as student recruiter	12.8	20.0	7.3	31.3
Departmental administrative duties	45.6	5.4	43.8	6.3
Participation in campus symposia	25.0	11.7	29.2	10.4

adviser to student organizations a "major factor," 12.5 percent of them consider it "not a factor." To 11.5 percent, willingness to teach undesirable courses is a "major factor," but 31.3 percent of the public college deans dismiss it as "not a factor."

Study Highlights

1. There is minimal change in the relative importance that academic deans accord factors in the evaluation of a professor's college service.
2. Service on collegewide committees and academic advising are cited by more academic deans than any other factor.
3. Service on department committees and department administrative duties continue as important considerations.
4. Liberal arts colleges assign least importance to willingness to teach undesirable courses and service as student recruiters.
5. Student advising and nonacademic student counseling receive greater recognition at private colleges than at public colleges.
6. Participation in campus symposia has picked up importance, especially at public colleges.

Conclusion: 1983 Study

Classroom teaching is the single most important consideration in evaluating faculty performance for purposes of tenure, promotion in rank, and retention — at least, that is the consensus reported by the deans of liberal arts colleges. But there is a nagging suspicion in many faculty members that other factors, particularly research and publication, pay off in administrative personnel decisions. Faculty doubts may be fueled by this study's findings that research, publication, and activities in professional societies have risen in recent years in the deans' estimation. They were considerably weightier in the 1983 study than in the writer's previous studies. Today, colleges pay closer attention to a professor's off-campus, discipline-related activities, which also happen to be the traditional hallmarks of academic success. A slow victim of this shifting emphasis, student advising, is becoming less important, although it is still a major consideration.

The study's findings also indicate that the entire evaluation process is becoming more structured and systematic. More data sources are being introduced, and the assessment procedures are more open. Although the department chairs and deans are still the predominant sources of information on teaching performance, their grip is loosening. Other data sources — classroom visits, course syllabi and examinations, and self-evaluation — are emerging in importance. Systematic student ratings have become so popular that today they closely trail dean evaluation in importance.

College policies and practices used to evaluate faculty scholarship/research are becoming more systematic. Books, monographs, journal articles, papers at professional meetings, even unpublished papers and reports — virtually all relevant information — are considered in the evaluation process. And the quality of all this work is judged mostly by peers at the institution, department chair, and academic dean and on the basis of the number and kind of professional honors or awards. The study indicates that public colleges in particular may be emphasizing research and publication in the drive to impress state legislatures and other public bodies that control the purse strings.

When it comes to evaluating college service, liberal arts colleges reserve their highest marks for service on collegewide and department committees and for academic advising and assuming departmental administrative duties. If academic advising has slipped a bit in the eyes of liberal arts colleges, participation in campus symposia has advanced in importance, especially in public colleges.

In short, some of the many changes in the way liberal arts colleges evaluate faculty performance may be trends, but they are not set in concrete, and the evaluative process must be continually challenged and steadily improved. The name of the game is improvement.

Chapter 4

Commentaries on the Causes and Implications of Changing Practices

Seven prominent educators were asked to comment on the significant changes revealed by the current study and specifically to respond to three questions: (1) Why have these changes taken place? (2) What are the implications for higher education? (3) What will faculty evaluation be like in the year 2000?

The Dynamics of Faculty Evaluation
by Lawrence M. Aleomoni

When a new Ph.D. graduate prepares to embark on a professional career at any one of the major universities in the United States or abroad, he or she is told by the department head or dean that the institution embraces the three general objectives of excellence in research, teaching, and service and that rewards are based on satisfactory to excellent performance in any one or a combination of those objectives. The sad fact is that after a short period of time at the institution, the new faculty member realizes that although the three objectives of research, teaching, and service are appropriate for any institution of higher education, most of the institutions reward faculty primarily for their performance in the research function.

Lawrence M. Aleomoni is professor of educational psychology and director of the Office of Instructional Research and Development at the University of Arizona.

This is a disturbing state of affairs, because it indicates, basically, that the institution is interested only in supporting and encouraging excellence in research. Its consequences are obvious in that faculty, regardless of their interest, may neglect their teaching and service activities in order to attain the professional recognition required to remain and succeed at their institution. Students are perhaps the most unfortunate pawns in such a game, since they are forced to take courses from faculty who are not able or willing to take the time to prepare and organize their courses or to do such things as spend time outside of class discussing problems and concerns that would help most students learn material better.

Some take the position that there is no inconsistency in this type of skewed reward system, since it is suggested that excellent researchers are, in fact, the best teachers. The research evidence, however, does not support this point and shows that, in general, there is no correlation between scholarly productivity and effective teaching.

It is further suggested that the evaluation of scholarly productivity is much easier, more valid, and more reliable than is the evaluation of instructional effectiveness. This attitude has generally resulted in a policy (dictated by practice) that, regardless of the quality of the evaluative teaching evidence, published research will still take precedence in the reward considerations. Under this policy, the relationship between teaching and scholarly productivity is believed to be high and positive, even though, as was stated above, the research evidence to date does not support this belief.

Faculty evaluation is typically based on assessment of performance in the research, teaching, and service areas and as such has been discussed, debated, maligned, and espoused by faculty, administrators, and students for some years now. The necessity of such evaluation is seldom questioned; however, the format and evidence used are frequently questioned. The actual elements used to evaluate faculty seem to have remained stable over the years. What seems to have changed, therefore, is the prominence of those elements within the three traditional categories of teaching, research, and service.

Ironically, the elements used to evaluate faculty in the teaching and service categories have retained their rank order of importance over the years in comparison to the elements in the research category. What this means is that chair evaluation, dean evaluation, and systematic student ratings are considered to be the three most frequently used sources of information (in that order) in evaluating teaching performance over the past five years, whereas books as sole or senior author, monographs or chapters in books, and books as junior author or editor were the three most frequently used in 1978, with books as sole or senior author, books as junior author or editor, and publication in all professional journals the three most frequently used in 1983.

This seeming stability of the order of evaluative elements in the teaching and service categories might indicate an objective, systematic approach to evaluation in each of those categories. Most of the published information on this subject, however, argues the opposite point of view and suggests that the evaluation of teaching has been subject to a wide variety of approaches, with no commonly accepted methods or techniques except for student judgments gathered via rating forms, some of which have not, admittedly, been professionally designed.

Since this study used academic deans at undergraduate liberal arts colleges to provide the data, one might conclude that they are either more realistic or more optimistic about the elements used to evaluate teaching performance than their faculty. For example, faculty are usually highly critical of the use of student ratings to evaluate their teaching performance. A careful perusal of the three most frequently used elements in evaluating teaching performance shows that two (chair and dean evaluation) represent the least documented and least representative forms of evaluation. Apparently, these administrators feel that their perceptions are accurate and that no documentation is necessary except for student ratings. Faculty, on the other hand, feel that student ratings are not accurate sources of information and, therefore, should not be used to judge their teaching performance. Implicit in all this is a basic belief on the part of administrators and faculty that the evaluation of teaching performance is more subjective, less reliable, and less accurate than the evaluation of research performance.

During the past ten years, several proposals have been advanced outlining how comprehensive and objective systems of instructional evaluation can be developed. This has resulted in a plethora of papers and symposia on the subject, not to mention its treatment in several new books on faculty evaluation. This information has apparently not gone unnoticed by deans and department heads, since this study shows significant increases in the use of systematic student ratings, self-evaluation or report, course syllabi and exams, and classroom visits over the past five years. In fact, when evaluators are asked to indicate what the major factors are in judging overall faculty performance, classroom teaching is cited first among comprehensive universities and colleges as well as doctorate-granting universities and second among research universities. It appears, therefore, that teaching effectiveness is the most prominent concern in evaluating faculty performance. If that is true, then why do faculty on university and college campuses nationwide feel that instructional efforts go unrewarded? The answer apparently is based on their personal experiences and perceptions. In a recent survey of 1,141 faculty members at the University of Arizona, 50 percent indicated that teaching is scarcely rewarded at all, 43 percent indicated that teaching is rewarded occasionally, and 7 percent indicated that teaching is well rewarded. In order to convince faculty that instructional effectiveness is an integral part of the institutional reward scheme, upper-level administration must require each department and/or college to develop a policy for valid evaluation of their instructional effort. In addition, upper-level administration must provide basic instructional services and resources that will convince faculty that instruction is, in fact, a valued and integral part of the institutional mission. By suggesting guidelines for departments to follow in establishing comprehensive systems of faculty evaluation, the administration will be able to convince faculty of their desire to produce an improved instructional and professional environment. All this attention to developing accurate means of evaluating faculty performance has coincided with a keen awareness that our educational system has not been doing an effective job of teaching students basic skills. It appears that, at long last, the public is becoming aware that unless we can accurately evaluate, improve, and reward instructional efforts, we will be faced with reaping crops of students with basic deficiencies in skills necessary for the survival of our way of life.

With respect to the future, I feel that faculty evaluation will be a very comprehensive, well-defined system by the year 2000, with explicit criteria and guidelines for evaluation decisions. These systems will be predominantly computer based, with explicit recommendations for improvement provided along with time lines to achieve improvement. There will be much less reliance on anecdotal and/or testimonial evidence and much more on objective, quantifiable evidence. Every new faculty member will be able to construct a contract indicating how much time and effort will be devoted to teaching, research, and service and what criteria will be used to judge his or her effectiveness in each of those areas. This will provide faculty members with the opportunity of tailoring their professional careers along the lines that best suit them rather than trying to fit a predetermined model. Such a climate will lead to more satisfied and productive faculty, who will be capable of delivering instruction and encouraging students to learn at levels heretofore unattained.

Evaluation of Faculty Performance: Key Issues
by Raoul A. Arreola

The evaluation of faculty is not a new phenomenon, yet it continues to elicit reactions in faculty ranging from cold apathy to heated anger. The reasons for these reactions are varied and complex. One reason stands out, however, and an examination of it may help illuminate some of the results of the study presented herein. The negative reactions to any situation arise when a conflict is present. The single most profound conflict in the area of faculty evaluation revolves around the fact that faculty are hired and receive their paychecks for doing one thing, teaching, but are promoted and tenured for doing another, research and publication. Thus, faculty are paid for teaching, but the amount they are paid and the rank they hold, as well as how secure they are in their position, depend on their doing research and publishing articles. This is an old and time-honored conflict, and the continuation of it has been nurtured by the persistent myth that one cannot be a good teacher without being a good researcher. All faculty are faced with the familiar problem of trying to carve out enough time

Raoul A. Arreola is chairperson of the Division of Education at the University of Tennessee Center for the Health Sciences.

to do both teaching and research when doing just one well can be an almost all-consuming activity. This situation has the elements of the classic "approach-approach" conflict familiar to sophomore psychology students. If the faculty member moves in one direction, he or she is penalized for not moving in the other, opposite, direction, and vice versa. In practice, we can see the faculty member who takes the time and effort to become a good teacher not having the time to write and do research in sufficient quantities and of sufficient quality to get promoted or tenured as quickly as those who do. Likewise, we can find faculty members who do considerable research and writing and then receive poor student ratings of their teaching and pay the penalties that brings. This is not to imply that a good teacher cannot be a good researcher, and vice versa. It is just that those who are good at both of these somewhat diverse and time-competing endeavors are the exception and not the rule. With this underlying conflict situation in mind, we can examine the results of the present study with a somewhat different perspective, which may permit a slightly more insightful interpretation of the data.

A number of significant changes that have occurred in the practice of evaluating faculty over the past five years are reflected in the data. For our purposes, I will focus on those changes that have occurred in the overall evaluation of faculty in general and in the evaluation of teaching in particular. As can be seen from Tables 4 and 5, classroom teaching has remained as the single most frequently cited major consideration in the overall evaluation of faculty. The reason for its prominence and its unchanging importance are obvious. That's what faculty are hired and paid for. However, there have been some interesting and important shifts in the relative frequency and importance of use of some of the other aspects of faculty performance in their overall evaluation. In the broadest sense, student advising, campus committee work, and length of service still outstrip research and publication as the most frequently utilized factors in overall faculty evaluation. However, there have been significant increases in the importance of research, publication, and activities in professional societies during the last five years, while there has been a significant decrease in the importance of personal attributes and student advising. Thus, although the emphasis on teaching is as strong as ever, there has been a growing emphasis on the importance of research, publication, and professional activity. The drop in the overall emphasis in the use and importance of personal attributes and the drop in the overall use of length of service in evaluating faculty speak to a trend to begin using more objective indicators of performance in this endeavor.

The relatively hard economic times in which higher education has found itself during the last five years have often resulted in administrators having to make decisions to dismiss or not tenure more faculty than has previously been the case. These actions implicitly threaten legal suits, which require much more objective measures of faculty performance than have traditionally been gathered. Not surprisingly, then, we find a growing emphasis on publication, research, and professional competence, as indicated by honors, awards, articles, books, and the use of peers from other institutions to provide this information (see Table 16).

Since the study results indicate that teaching is of preeminent importance and use, I would like to focus the remainder of my comments on this dimension. As can be seen in Tables 9 and 10, departmental chairs, deans, and systematic student ratings are the most frequently used and most important sources of information in evaluating teaching. These are followed at some distance by committee evaluations, colleague opinions, and self-evaluations in both importance and frequency of use. These conditions have not changed appreciably over the last five years. However, there have been a few significant changes with profound implications that should be examined. Most notably, as can be seen in Table 10, there has been a significant increase in the importance of student ratings, self-evaluation, course syllabi and examinations, and classroom visits in the evaluation of teaching. Likewise, there has been a decrease in the importance of informal student ratings. All of these changes are in keeping with the overall trend to gather evaluative data that are more objective and perhaps more legally defensible. It is interesting to note the significant increase in the importance and use of self-evaluations, since, by their very nature, self-evaluations contribute little in an overall faculty evaluation program. Very few individuals will give themselves poor evaluations, and those that do deserve them. Thus, self-evaluations can serve only to either place the other evaluations into a somewhat better context or simply permit the faculty member to "tell his side." In any case, it is apparent that this change has most likely been brought about more in the interests of political and legal necessity than for the purposes of more objective measurement.

The other changes that have occurred since 1978 — notably, the significant increases in the importance and frequency of use of student ratings, course syllabi and examinations, and classroom visits — offer evidence of a more profound and potentially important change. These changes, especially the changes relating to the use and importance of course syllabi and examinations, signal a fundamental shift toward a more complete understanding and, thus, evaluation of the act of teaching.

Traditionally, good teachers have been defined as those who are competent in their content fields. This has long been the heart of the myth noted above that a person can be good as a teacher only if he or she is good as a researcher. However, the skills, training, and talents necessary to be a good researcher in a given subject are not automatically those necessary to be a good teacher. One activity is essentially a solitary, cognitive endeavor, while the other is essentially a social as well as affective and cognitive activity. Fundamentally, research requires the manipulation of materials and ideas, while teaching requires the manipulation of minds and attributes as well as ideas. Thus the "approach-approach" conflict noted earlier may be further complicated by a deeper "approach-avoidance" conflict. That is, someone trained to a solitary, cognitive activity such as research may not necessarily enjoy having to engage in a social, manipulative activity such as teaching, even though he or she has to do it to get paid.

It is appropriate to take a closer look at the underlying dimensions of teaching so as to gain a more complete appreciation for what the shift in the use of course syllabi and examinations, classroom visitation, and student ratings over the past five years implies.

Teaching can be thought of as encompassing three broad dimensions: content expertise, instructional delivery skills, and instructional design skills. Content expertise can be defined as that body of skills, competencies, and knowledge in a specific area in which the faculty member has received advanced training and education. In evaluating this component, it is obvious that either peers or department chairpersons would be the most logical and appropriate sources of information. Since teaching traditionally has been thought of as being composed almost entirely of this component, it is not surprising to find department chairperson as well as committee or colleague opinion high on the list of sources used in evaluating teaching. In addition, since students, by definition, would not be competent to evaluate the content expertise of a faculty member, we must explain the increase in use of student ratings in some other way. If we look at the second broad dimension of teaching, instructional delivery skills, we can gain an insight into this increase. Instructional delivery skills can be defined as those human interactive skills and characteristics that promote or facilitate learning by creating an appropriate learning environment. Such characteristics as enthusiasm, ability to motivate, and ability to capture and hold the interest and attention of students are included, as well as the ability to engender an overall agreeable learning environment appropriate to the content being taught. For this dimension, we can generally consider students competent to report their reactions to the performance characteristics of the faculty member relative to classroom presentations. Students can appropriately be asked to rate those human interactive skills and characteristics that in and of themselves do not produce learning but rather create an environment or affective situation that promotes and facilitates it. Such ratings have been shown to be reliable and, when taken in the correct context, valid. The increase in the use and importance of student ratings reflected in the study results tends to imply a greater acceptance and recognition of the value of students' input on this dimension. However, the concomitant increase in classroom visitation would also tend to imply that department chairpersons, deans, or whoever is doing the visiting also wish to gain some firsthand evidence of the instructor's instructional delivery skills.

Finally, we come to the third dimension, instructional design skills. This dimension can be divided into two parts. The first part consists of those skills and competencies required to design effective instructional experiences and the strategies necessary to properly sequence and present those experiences so as to induce learning in the student. The second part consists of those skills and competencies necessary to accurately measure and confirm that learning has indeed occurred. If *instruction* is defined as an activity that induces learning, and if *learning* is defined as a specified change in the behavior of the student that must persist and be measurable, then the instructor must possess the skills necessary to execute these tasks correctly. Such skills as designing tests, preparing syllabi, handouts, learning objectives, and other such supportive materials, or properly utilizing media and other forms of instructional technology, as well as organizing lectures and presentations for maximal instructional impact, are included in this dimension. Taken in this context, it is apparent that the increase in the use of syllabi and course examinations as more important indicators of effective teaching implies a growing awareness of the importance the instructional design skills dimension has in the overall act of teaching.

During the last decade, we have seen a sharp decline in the mobility of university faculty. We have seen larger and larger budget cuts in higher education, resulting in a situation that makes promotion and tenure more and more difficult to attain. Just holding on to your job has, in many cases, supplanted the goal of getting that promotion or pay increase. Merit pay has withered, in many cases, to a fond memory. Over this same period, faculty evaluation programs have sprouted and spread all over the country. Originally designed as systems to provide feedback to faculty for self-improvement, these systems have been transformed into mechanisms used by administrators to make personnel decisions. State legislators are demanding more and more accountability for the shrinking tax dollars they are spending on education. All of these factors are bound to persist into the next century. Thus, we should see much more in the way of faculty evaluation, rather than less. However, the results of the present study tend to indicate that there may be some positive fundamental changes in the evaluation process. Primary among these is the implication of the growing recognition of a more multidimensional nature to teaching. Although the emphasis on research and publication continues to grow, teaching still dominates the faculty evaluation picture and will undoubtedly do so well into the future. In fact, with the growing trend toward competency testing before graduation in high schools and colleges, higher education should begin to experience a new commitment to quality teaching. In order for this commitment to be fully realized, however, fundamental changes in the reward structures of colleges and universities will have to take place. It must become possible for faculty to be promoted, tenured, and given merit raises on the basis of excellence in teaching. There must be a recognition that teaching, when undertaken seriously, with excellence as its goal, is a complex, time-consuming activity equal to research and publication and deserving of equally stringent evaluation efforts.

Better Faculty Evaluation Systems
by Judith D. Aubrecht

Peter Seldin invites comments on the changes in faculty evaluation practices in four-year, undergraduate liberal arts colleges, as reflected in a comparison between his 1978 and 1983 surveys. Seldin asks: (1) Why have these significant changes taken place? (2) What are the implications for higher education? (3) What will faculty evaluation be like in the year 2000?

I feel the need to reinterpret and reorder these questions — to make them my own — starting with "What will faculty evaluation be like in the year 2000?" The obvious answer is, "A lot better than it is now." The world of higher education is attending to this important task — reading books, going to seminars and conferences, meeting in committees to design new evaluation systems and to revise old ones. It has to get better. Therefore, the real question must be, "What constitutes better faculty evaluation?" The answers to this question, many of which are already known, provide a framework within which we can ask, "Do the Seldin surveys provide evidence of movement in the right directions?" I believe that the surveys demonstrate mostly positive change, along with an occasional wrong turn. Unfortunately, some of the relevant issues are not addressed by the surveys. Here I will ven-

Judith D. Aubrecht is administrator of the Center for Faculty Evaluation and Development at Kansas State University.

ture some "informed opinion" gathered while working with
various institutions as they develop and revise faculty evaluation
systems and while running center seminars on faculty evaluation
and instructional development for higher education personnel.

So, on with it: What constitutes better faculty evaluation
practice? First, faculty evaluation should be *systematic* (organized,
standardized), *comprehensive* (taking into account the wide range of
responsibilities for each individual), *public* (with known criteria
and procedures), and *flexible* (designed to accommodate change
and take advantage of the individual's talents and capabilities as
well as to serve the needs of the academic unit).

Although the Seldin surveys are not specifically designed to
reflect on these characteristics, it is clear that the movement
toward more *systematic* and *public* faculty evaluation practice is
inevitable. The idiosyncratic and impressionistic "let-the-dean-
do-it" days are over. Tables 4 and 5 of the surveys provide evidence of more *comprehensive* practice by demonstrating an increase
in the evaluation of most faculty responsibilities. Up significantly
is the evaluation of research, publication, and activity in professional societies. Also up, at least a bit, is the evaluation of supervision of graduate study (rather an odd category for this population), supervision of honors programs, public service, consultation, and campus committee work. The evaluation of only one
faculty responsibility, student advising, is down significantly.
Factors listed in the tables that are *not* responsibilities — length of
service in rank, competing job offers, and personal attributes —
are all down, with personal attributes down significantly. This is
an appropriate de-emphasis of nonperformance characteristics in
the evaluation of academic personnel.

The surveys do not offer evidence related to *flexibility*. It
seems likely, however, that this ultimately desirable characteristic
will have to await later refinements in most systems. The prior
needs for systematic, comprehensive, and public practice are perceived as at least partially in conflict with flexibility. (The first
approximation to a fair system is to treat everyone in the same
way.) Eventually, accommodations will evolve within the systems
that will also optimize the individual's contribution to the institution and individual opportunities for growth.

Better faculty evaluation practice would acknowledge, clarify, and resolve conflicts related to the concepts of *merit, worth,* and *market value.* These ideas have had some limited discussion in the literature (Scriven, 1978; Aubrecht and Kramer, 1982). Faculty evaluation has traditionally been based on *merit,* excellence in research and teaching. These are characteristics of the individual faculty member. (Of course, it is possible to think of the merit of the institution as it reflects collective faculty quality.) *Worth* has to do with value to the institution. Worth requires merit, but merit is not a sufficient condition for worth. When an institution eliminates an excellent program (and dismisses the people working in the program) because of "financial exigency," it is making a decision about worth, not about merit. Worth, then, is a characteristic of the interaction between the quality of the faculty member and the needs of the institution. *Market value* is a function of worth in the outside world. To lure a physician away from private medical practice or a computer scientist away from industry is to confront the issue of market value. It makes little sense (once you understand the impact of market value) to claim that medical school faculty or computer-science faculty are "no better than" teachers of English or history and therefore should be paid the same (a merit argument). Nor does it make sense to say that English teachers and history teachers typically work with more students per term than do teachers of computer science or medicine and therefore should be paid more (a worth argument). A college can either pay physicians and computer scientists more or forget about having a medical school or a computer-science department.

By specifying the part each of these concepts — merit, worth, and market value — plays in faculty evaluation, it is at least possible to reduce some of the misunderstandings and hostilities. That is, it is clearly *desirable* to evaluate faculty on the basis of excellence (merit) and thus acknowledge that English faculty are "as good as" medical faculty. At the same time, it is *necessary* to reward faculty financially on the basis of worth and market value. (Acknowledge my national reputation as a Renaissance scholar and my ability to inspire graduate students, even if you do not pay me as well as you do the average professor in a more marketable field.) Merit, worth, and market value are not addressed in the Seldin surveys. Nor are they yet incorporated openly in evaluation systems. They should be (and long before the year 2000).

Better faculty evaluation systems would collect data efficiently to serve many purposes (for example, personnel decision making, faculty development, program evaluation), while at the same time keeping the evaluation and development functions appropriately distinct. Under no circumstances should information promised to faculty members strictly for instructional improvement be subsequently turned over to those who make decisions about promotion, tenure, retention/termination, or salary increases. The Seldin surveys do not provide evidence for changed practice here. However, I feel quite safe in saying that very few institutions are making good use of their faculty evaluation systems for development purposes. At the same time, too many institutions allow their personnel decision-making procedures to interfere with (subvert) their development activities. The prime example of this is the still-increasing use of colleague visits to the classroom for evaluating teaching. This is notoriously bad practice, as will be explained later, in the discussion on reliability. Even worse than bad evaluation practice is the consequent destruction of an excellent potential tool for instructional improvement. Systematic classroom observation and feedback to teachers of *descriptive* information (what is happening in the classroom, not whether it is good or bad) is an extremely effective and reliable development process (Hyman, 1968; Acheson and Gall, 1980; Aubrecht, 1978). Classroom observation should be used only for development. It is very disturbing that the Seldin surveys indicate an increased use of classroom visits for the evaluation of teaching performance.

Better faculty evaluation systems would employ a variety of types of data (for example, survey questionnaires, interviews, course materials, samples of student work, publications, citation indices). The Seldin surveys do suggest progress in this area, including significantly greater use of systematic student ratings, course syllabi and examinations, and most of the types of data used to evaluate research. The occasional decreases in the use of a particular type of data, notably informal student opinions and enrollments in elective courses, make sense in terms of the relative reliability and validity of the data type. (The issues of reliability and validity will be discussed below.)

Better faculty evaluation practice would collect information from many sources (for example, students, colleagues, department heads, members of community service groups, and the faculty members themselves) and would make clearer distinctions between the sources or suppliers of the data and the users of the data. The people closest to the activity being assessed are generally in the best position to supply relevant information. (For example, it makes no sense to ask a department head to provide information on Professor X's service to the local recycling group. Ask the president of the recycling group.) The users of the data are determined by the purpose of the evaluation. (The department head uses the information supplied by the president of the recycling group to judge Professor X's community service. The faculty member is the user of the data if it is collected for instructional improvement.) The Seldin surveys do not clearly reflect whether there is actually an increase in the variety of sources of information or whether more people are doing the evaluating (using the data). The surveys simply mirror the great confusion in many institutions over this very basic point.

Better faculty evaluation systems would be increasingly data based. They would attend to issues of reliability and validity that have so far been addressed in any substantial way only in the research on student ratings of instruction. The fundamental questions will need to be answered for other sources and types of data used in faculty evaluation. An illustration from the student rating literature seems worthwhile here. The basic questions are: (1) Are student ratings reliable? Do they measure consistently whatever they measure? (2) Are student ratings valid? Do they measure what they ought to measure for the purposes they serve? Ratings commonly serve two purposes — evaluation for personnel decision making and information for instructional development. If student ratings are valid for evaluation purposes, then students should rate higher those courses and teachers from whom they learn more. If they are valid for development, they should provide useful suggestions for improving instruction.

There are additional important validity questions: (1) Are

student ratings biased? Are they affected by extraneous factors that are not under the control of the teacher? If so, can these factors be identified, and can their impact be eliminated, either procedurally (by standardizing the administration of the forms) or statistically (by adjusting for known systematic biases after the ratings are collected)? (2) Do student ratings agree with ratings of other relevant groups? Do colleagues, administrators, the instructors themselves, and alumni agree with the ratings given by students? (3) Are student ratings generalizable? How many courses taught by an instructor (and how many sections within a course) should be sampled in order to make adequate predictions of future teaching effectiveness?

There is insufficient space here (nor is it the purpose of this commentary) to supply evidence from the literature to demonstrate satisfying answers to each of these questions (although we would be happy to provide such references for the interested reader). The important point is that reliability and validity questions must also be asked of other forms of data used in faculty evaluation (for example, colleague ratings of course materials, student ratings of academic advising, peer ratings of published works).

The Seldin surveys do provide some evidence of movement toward more reliable and valid forms of data and away from the weaker forms: toward systematic student ratings, reviews of course materials and examinations, and reviews of publications, citations, and papers presented at national meetings, all at least likely to be acceptably reliable and valid data types; away from informal student opinion, enrollment in elective courses, and ratings of personal attributes, all of somewhat more dubious value.

There are two notable instances of movement in the wrong directions. The first is the increase in classroom visits for evaluating teaching, already discussed above. This is an extremely unreliable practice; colleagues just do not agree in their evaluations of classroom practice (Centra, 1975). (If you believe that this *can* be done reliably, just get a group of faculty and/or administrators together, play an audio or video segment of a real class, and have people discuss it. Every center seminar on instructional development includes this activity. There are always people in the seminar who think the instructor is excellent and others who believe he is incompetent.)

The second wrong direction is the increased use of scholarly research and publication as a factor in evaluating teaching performance (no problem with its use in evaluating overall performance, of course). There is almost no correlation between teaching performance and research productivity (Centra, 1981). Therefore, research productivity cannot be a valid measure of teaching performance.

In sum, faculty evaluation practice *is* improving. The Seldin surveys provide direct evidence for greater comprehensiveness, the increased evaluation of almost all faculty responsibilities, as well as a decrease in the evaluation of nonperformance characteristics. They also demonstrate a greater variety of types (and perhaps sources) of data and a movement toward those types and sources of data that are likely to be adequately reliable and valid. Further improvements will inevitably include (1) the elimination of classroom observation for evaluation, (2) the elimination of research productivity as a factor in the evaluation of teaching, (3) increased opportunities for faculty development, along with greater separation of the evaluation and development functions, and (4) research into the reliability and validity of sources and types of data similar to those currently available for student ratings of instruction.

Faculty Evaluation: Problems and Solutions
by Arthur W. Chickering

The days of benign neglect and seat-of-the pants evaluation of faculty performance are fast disappearing. Just as public pressures for more rigorous evaluation of student performance are rapidly increasing, so also are public pressures for institutional accountability and professional performance. These external pressures are amplified by two conditions that will persist for the foreseeable future. First, institutional enrollments and budgets will remain steady or decline in most colleges and universities. Under this steady-state condition, improving quality means investing more heavily in faculty development for persons already

Arthur W. Chickering is Distinguished Professor of Higher Education and director of the Center for the Study of Higher Education at Memphis State University.

employed, most of whom are tenured. If effective professional development programs are to be carried out with such experienced and entrenched faculty members, then they will have to rest on tough-minded evaluation of faculty performance. Second, although overall enrollments and dollar support seem likely to remain steady, there will be enrollment shifts within each institution as changes in the workplace and larger social changes influence student motives and interest. Many institutions have been trying to reallocate resources from colleges of education and from arts and sciences to colleges of business and engineering. And departments within colleges wax and wane. When these enrollment shifts have to be addressed in a steady-state context, with high proportions of tenured professionals, faculty evaluation becomes critical. And such evaluation cannot simply rest with whether or not a faculty member is doing an excellent, good, or mediocre job in his or her area of primary expertise or current employment. Evaluation must stretch to assess whether that person has other areas of competence that can be employed to meet the heavier enrollment pressures in other areas. These conditions, entirely new in the history of higher education, challenge mightily our current and past approaches to faculty evaluation.

Most of us who have hung around higher education for any length of time are aware of the problems besetting faculty evaluation. First, there is the gap between what Chris Argyris would call our "espoused theory" and our "theory in use." Our espoused theory says that faculty responsibilities include service, teaching, and research. We also assert that evaluation of teaching weighs as heavily on our judgments as evaluation of research. However, in our heart of hearts, those of us who have been close to the evaluation process know that, come promotion and tenure time in most institutions, first consideration is given to research and publication. If those criteria are satisfied, and if there is no significant difference among candidates, then teaching effectiveness comes into play. Finally, a nod may be given to service contributions.

But even if we should get our theory in use more congruent with our espoused theories, so teaching and service are given more appropriate weights, two difficult problems remain. These are the problems of criteria and evidence. What criteria do we employ to make judgments about effective teaching? Do we assess the amount of learning that occurs among students, the "value added" in knowledge, competence, and personal development that occurs in our courses? Do we evaluate the degree to which knowledge and competence demonstrated at the end of a course or the gains that have occurred are retained? For how long? A semester? A year? Until graduation? Beyond graduation? What are reasonable expectations concerning the amount of learning or gain that might occur in a single course? And how do these expectations need to vary given the prior ability, knowledge, competence, and experiences of students? Is a large gain by a relatively poor student to be given more weight than a small gain by a very bright, well-prepared student?

If we come to terms with the complex judgments concerning criteria for good, bad, and indifferent performance and with the value issues behind them, then the problem of appropriate and sound evidence remains. We recognize that, while student ratings of teacher performance provide useful information, they do not provide sound evidence concerning learning that may or may not have occurred. Would some kind of pre- and postassessment be a useful addition? Can we assess the complex outcomes we value most highly? Are there the institutional resources, professional expertise, time, and dollars available to undertake such evaluation? If such expertise and resources are not going to be available, are there some proxy indicators, some "unobtrusive measures" that might be identified? The point is that, with the best will and with appropriate weight given to teaching in relation to research, tough problems concerning criteria and evidence remain.

Then, of course, there are the persistent problems of internal politics, ideological conflicts, and personality clashes. These agendas, sometimes hidden, sometimes not so hidden, influence our judgments more often than we care to recognize. They operate at the department, college, and university levels. More objective, systematic, and rigorous faculty evaluation can provide leverage against such forces, but those forces, like a low-level infection, will be ready to come into play when a decision must be made about a cantankerous, abrasive colleague, no matter how excellent the performance.

Our steady-state enrollments and budgets, accompanied by internal shifts, and the primitive, impressionistic nature of current faculty evaluation procedures provide the context for considering the findings reported in this book. What do these findings suggest about where we are and where we are going? What changes seem to be occurring? Why are they taking place?

The major factors used in evaluating overall faculty performance are teaching, student advising, campus committee work, length of service, personal attributes, and research. No major surprises there. In the five years from 1978 to 1983, increased attention was being given to research, publication, and activity in professional societies, while student advising and personal attributes were less frequently taken into account. Do these shifts reflect a movement toward more easily measured, publicly accessible, noncontroversial criteria and data, as administrators have to make increasingly difficult decisions concerning tenure/promotion? That is one hypothesis worth testing.

The key sources of information used, in rank order, are chair evaluation, dean evaluation, systematic student ratings, committee evaluation, colleagues' opinions, and self-evaluation or report. The sources of information least frequently used are perhaps more instructive: enrollment in elective courses, long-term follow-up of students, and student examination performance. Thus, it is the opinions of chairpersons, deans, colleagues, and committees, leavened by student rating, that dominate the information on which judgments are based, rather than data concerning student performance and student behavior in terms of "voting with their feet." In this regard, it is worth noting that classroom visits and course syllabi and examinations are also used to only a very modest degree. The changes suggest that we are reaching for more substantive information. Use of classroom visits, systematic student ratings, course syllabi and examinations, and self-evaluations increased significantly. Enrollment in elective courses dropped, but perhaps that is a function of reductions in the number of electives available and increased student concern to meet external requirements. Such shifts make that variable less available as a useful source of information. The data suggest that as administrators, colleagues, and committees face increasingly difficult decisions, they are seeking information more directly related to teaching effectiveness.

The types of information used in evaluating scholarship and research — books and publication in professional journals — yield no surprises. Nor does the emphasis given to judgments by department chairpersons, peers at the institution, and the academic dean, in addition to honors and awards from the profession. But the changes concerning judgments about the quality of research are interesting. In rank order, they are referee or editor of a professional journal, grants or funding received, self-evaluation, honors or awards, and peers at *other* institutions. Judgments by department chairpersons, peers at one's own institution, and the academic dean remain unchanged. Once again, the changes observed suggest increased efforts to obtain added information, and information of a kind which is more objective, provided by sources outside the institution, and presumably more free from local professional biases and political considerations.

The two major factors used in evaluating service were academic advising and service on collegewide committees. Service on department committees and departmental administrative duties came next but were much less frequently used. Participation in campus symposia was the only response option to show change, reflected a slight increase in frequency. It may be worth noting that off-campus services — to the local community, to the state or region, to national or international councils, boards, agencies, and the like — either were not included as response alternatives or were noted so infrequently as not to be included in the data summaries.

What do these findings suggest, and what do they imply for the future? To me, they suggest the early stages of a healthy effort to obtain more information, and more objective information, for evaluating faculty performance in teaching and in research. These changes are certainly in the right direction. To have sound systems of faculty evaluation and faculty development to improve the quality of education, we need information that is (1) as objective as possible, (2) obtained through clearly articulated methods and processes, which are (3) public accessible, not at the level of data concerning individuals but at the level of agreed-upon content, methods, and criteria. We need to move toward "third-party" evaluations that enrich and temper the perspectives of local administrators and peers. We need to move away from the private, unarticulated, impressionistic data and methods that weigh heavily in most current systems for faculty evaluation.

Local administrators and peer review committees will always need to retain authority and responsibility for the final recommendations and judgments that are made. But those local judgments need strengthening by more hard-nosed empirical data and by sophisticated third-party appraisals. Ultimately, the quality of our professional performance and the value of our professional development program to improve that performance will depend heavily on the rigor and soundness of our evaluative information and on its acceptance by the professionals with whom it is employed and the soundness of the local judgments that are made. If we can significantly improve our activities concerning faculty evaluation and development, then we will also significantly improve our capacity to meet the legitimate pressures for increased accountability and improved performance.

New Directions in Faculty Evaluation
by Kenneth E. Eble

In the time I have been an observer of faculty evaluation, I have seen it steadily move to more care in gathering data, more attention to ruling out prejudice and subjectivity, and more involvement of those actually affected by the process. When I entered faculty ranks in 1955, the "clubby" aspects of evaluation were still present, even at a middling sort of state university. My first department chairman *did* visit classes of new faculty members, and he was the source of most of the specific information about a faculty member's performance. We did not have student evaluation data— that didn't begin in my university until 1968 — and the discussions among peers that were crucial to advancement, then as now, were

Kenneth E. Eble is professor of English and former chairperson of the English department at the University of Utah.

strongly affected by opinions based on scanty evidence. This was particularly true of teaching, where casual praise from a single student or a casual impression of a public performance could pass for substantial evidence. In scholarship, there was conscientious reading of printed work but little searching beyond that to assess scholarly virtue in those who didn't publish or to test work much beyond its acceptance by specialized journals. To my mind, there was a saving looseness in our procedures. The collective judgments were probably better than any single person's, and the collegiality maintained as a virtue then may have sanctioned mediocrity, but in exchange for a decent working atmosphere for a wider range of talents and interests.

Peter Seldin's work provides a measure of change over the past decade — an important measure, for there is a dividing line between many practices in academia as they were from shortly after World War II until 1970 and as they have been since. The greater care and systematization of evaluation arise from a number of causes. Economic pressures create and sustain a demand for accountability. The growth of faculty power — as in unionization, on one hand, and shared governance, on the other — increases the demand for a visible and equitable (by faculty measures) evaluation system. The expansion of faculty itself has made more personal, collegial procedures obsolete. Indeed, one could argue that changing conditions in higher education quickly manifest themselves in faculty evaluation.

Three examples will illustrate this claim. Student evaluation, which bumbled along here and there for at least three decades (even excepting the war years), established itself with remarkable swiftness from the late sixties on. Its use is still increasing and, I think, for a variety of reasons. But its becoming firmly established against strong faculty resistance is surely traceable to the changes effected by the great influx of students in the sixties. The 1983 survey reveals almost as clearly the presence of a highly competitive academic market, as well as a return to what a majority of faculty probably regard as "traditional" values. I refer to the increasing weight given to research, publication, and professional activities and to the increasing use of outside referees of scholarly productivity, as well as to less attention being given to advising, committee work, and personal attributes. Add to this the fact that teaching also seems to be scrutinized more closely—not only by student evaluations, but also by class visits and examining of course materials—and a reasonable approximation emerges of a market in which jobs are hard to get and hard to hang on to. A third reflection is in the increased defensiveness in evaluation procedures, which may mirror an increasingly litigious academic atmosphere, one in which trust and collegiality have greatly eroded. Chairpersons, for example, at many institutions no longer preside over or even furnish information to review committees. Tangible measures of judgment get preference, not because they may be better, but because they afford written evidence that may stand up in court.

Even in making these few observations, I am struck by gains and losses in the way faculty evaluation has changed. In general, more identifying of useful data, more care in gathering that data and in using it in informed discussion, and some diffusion of decision-making power seem mostly to the good. Nevertheless, some of the ease that goes with more casual procedures carried out by someone we trust is sacrificed in this change. In general, a crucial fact of faculty evaluation is that the more rigorous it becomes, the more it creates a desire of the faculty to play a strong part, and the greater become the demands on faculty members' time. There is no way around this, and I think it creates a major problem for faculty evaluation in the years ahead. How much time can faculty invest in evaluating each other without its becoming counterproductive? Following from that broad question are such specific questions as: What data is most valuable, and how does that value relate to the faculty time taken to gather it? What are minimum procedures to ensure an adequate measure of rigor and fairness? What part of evaluation can be turned over to others: students, administrators, evaluation experts?

As yet, I think there are gains in greater faculty involvement and in using student input. Both help to increase the attention being given to just what we are trying to accomplish by our valuing of specific competences. In respect to weighting the value of diverse aspects of faculty performance, I think little has changed. The question is a crucial one and may cause as much dissatisfaction with evaluation processes as any single part of these procedures. As institutions have become larger and more diverse, it has become necessary to provide within a faculty for more diverse services. Remedial instruction is but one example of work that carries low prestige, seldom results in respected publication, and stands in the way of conventional academic career advancement. Yet such work must be performed; it can stand for all the variety of necessary functions that are performed, often at high levels of competence, but that are outweighed by both conventional research and teaching. Moreover, the value attached to teaching rises with the level of classes being taught. At the bottom are remedial and freshman work; at the top, the graduate seminar. Very little has been done to break away from this perceived value structure, inapplicable as it may be on many campuses. The three-legged stool—research, teaching, service—never sat very firmly. It totters even more today.

If evaluation is to improve greatly, it must continue to wrestle strenuously with the prior questions of what an institution values and rewards. Responses to a survey on teaching evaluation at the University of California provide some provocative data. Within such a research-oriented university, it is not surprising that faculty and chairpersons were in almost exact agreement that on a 100-point scale, the desirable emphasis to be given to teaching is 31 points; to research and creative work, 43 points; to professional competence and activity, 16 points; to university and public service, 11 points. These are faculty figures. Respective figures for chairpersons are 32, 41, 15, and 12. A difference is evident, however, in what faculty and chairpersons believed the actual emphasis to be at the University of California. Faculty saw teaching as worth only 20 points, chairpersons saw it as worth 27; faculty saw research and creative work as worth 57 points, and contrasted with chairpersons' 48. Faculty believed other services to be slightly undervalued as compared with chairpersons' views.

The obvious reflection here is that teaching and service at this kind of university are accepted as weighing less than research and creative work and professional activity. But what is also revealed is that chairpersons perceive a closer balance between these two kinds of activities than do faculty. The common plaint of "publish or perish" resides to some degree in these differences of perception. However well evaluation is done, the results in terms of impact on faculty are conditioned by the weighting given to different faculty activities.

What is not revealed in this survey is that these generalized figures about four accepted categories of service fail to take into account the diversity of valuable services faculty actually perform. The assumption by both faculty and administration is that every faculty member will be good to whatever desirable degree in all of these general categories. But here, both the nature of individual talent and interest and the varied demands placed on colleges and universities argue for greater differentiation. Few colleges and universities wrestle strenuously with this problem, though contracting arrangements recognize it. Under yearly "contract" systems, a faculty member and chairperson agree upon what emphasis is to be given to what services during a coming period, and evaluation is made on that basis. Thus, a faculty member may be able to give greatest attention to teaching at one time, to research at another. Moreover, faculty doing the necessary work of a department may be judged by how well they do that work rather than by general standards. Such contracting arrangements work in some places and do not in others. But the need to reach agreements about just what services are expected and how much they are valued is fundamental to evaluation.

My final observation is a hope that such books as this, which draw attention to the facts of evaluation, will help to stimulate reflection about some of the larger implications. For evaluating faculty, like grading students, surely has other ends than culling and classifying and certifying. The linkages between evaluating and motivating—for faculty as for students—need to be continually explored. And the enhancement of a broad and humane learning for both faculty and students needs to be kept out there as that vital abstraction that justifies all this constant peering at each other.

The Context of Evaluation
by George L. Geis

People in many organizations would not be shocked if they were asked to answer these questions: What do you do, exactly? How well do you do it? How does what you do contribute to the goals of your organization? Professors, however, are likely to respond to these inquiries with disbelief and anger.

Both basic and applied research in the evaluation of professors are necessary and welcome. Peter Seldin continues his contribution to this area in this book. But research in evaluation, its application to practice, and the reactions to the application must be understood in the context of a dramatically changing academe, for evaluation as it is conceived of today is a relatively new phenomenon. Permit me to present, in capsule form, a fanciful description of the recent changes in the campus environment that have occurred concurrently with the changes in evaluation.

The Context: From Monastery to Industry. In the past three decades, postsecondary education has experienced an extended period of explosive growth of resources, personnel, and students, followed by a sudden drastic reduction in funds, decline in enrollments, and close to a ban on hiring new professors. The period of expansion changed the structures and means of governance in many institutions. The importance, methods, uses, and perceptions of evaluation have changed concurrently.

After World War II, the traditional model of the college or university was still in place. It resembled in many ways that of a monastery. A group of dedicated, otherworldly, underpaid, and somewhat socially deviant males — acolytes of knowledge — loosely banded together to pursue individual, isolated, and often esoteric searches for understanding and enlightenment. They engaged in scholarship, and they taught the young.

Each professor's commitment was to his own learning and, through it, to his discipline. His institution was a vehicle that permitted him to pursue his interests, to grow throughout a lifetime

George L. Geis is a member (and former director) of the Centre for Teaching and Learning Services at McGill University.

according to his own pattern. That growth was almost totally self-governed and self-monitored. Like a good Victorian child, he knew what was expected of him; he had internalized the rules and systems of control. After all, most professors (and many students) had come from similar family backgrounds and gone to similar schools.

Professors came together when absolutely necessary to govern the community. *Govern* may be too strong a word; the objective was to maintain an environment that allowed and encouraged individual, idiosyncratic pursuits. Concern was usually with preventing infringement upon that freedom and maintaining vague standards while aiming at ambiguous goals — and, of course, discussing at length eternal questions of parking spaces and cafeteria food.

The machinery of governance was centered around faculty meetings (or representations of them, such as senates). The organizational chart was bland and flat, marked only by a few perturbations, such as deans and chairs — positions painfully, unenthusiastically filled by those who had been tapped by their peers to serve time. Financial crises, which occurred rarely in the limited, stable economy of the institution, were generally handled by a group of paternalistic philanthropists — the board of trustees. In short, it was a peaceful picture of a group of isolates who agreed to come together in order to preserve their isolated ways.

Accountability? Evaluation? Careful selection acted to populate the campus with responsible, self-monitoring professors — or so the story goes. (Recent data on faculty stress suggest that the professoriate is still composed of self-judging, high-achieving individuals.) One's peers, when necessary, would decide if a candidate was worthy of entrance or continued membership in the community — much like the methods used in other fine men's clubs.

Certainly it was hoped that the consequence of the system would be excellence in teaching and research. Accountability for that achievement was clearly to one's self and one's peers. Small faculties and small student bodies encouraged feedback about teaching. The same students were in classes throughout a department, promoting discussions and comparisons of teachers. An informal subtle control system could operate.

Crushing in upon this bucolic environment was growth, a logarithmic expansion. And with it came a very different model — an industrial model; education was big business. Warning tremors after World War II included the expansion and increased heterogeneity not only of the student body but also of the faculty, the development of hierarchical systems of governance, the growing number of nonacademics in "administrative" positions, the weakening of faculty control over decision making, and the vastly increased number of important decisions to be made and made quickly. Often such decisions involved intricate interactions with off-campus agencies (for example, government funding units). Major quakes began to occur when reductions in budgets became serious and obvious.

Higher education had become an industry concerned with searching out raw materials (for example, students, research money), processing them, and turning out products. Persons involved in the industry began to be viewed as employers or employees, with a rift appearing between administrators and faculty members. Professors, unbelievably, even unionized. Discussions in faculty clubs (membership had become deductible in some places as a business expense) were of salaries, fringe benefits, and security. The life of a professor had become a job. Noxious gases of evaluation began to issue from the fissures and vents. Indeed, what would be more reasonable than to ask workers the questions posed at the opening of this paper?

Unpleasant though evaluation might be, it was hardly a potentially lethal threat as long as the decision process was peppered with *and* options. If a professor did not seem to be a good teacher, his or her deficiency could be remedied by adding another — teaching-oriented — staff member or a few teaching assistants. Five or so years ago, *and* decisions began to be replaced by *or* decisions. Finite, drastically reduced funding required that the solution of a problem reduce the resources available for the solution of others. Everyday operations and future planning began with consideration of budgetary constraints. "Which one" replaced "how many." And evaluation became serious.

It was accurate to portray evaluation as a vapor. It has been shifting and ambiguous. In the 1960s, evaluation, especially the evaluation of teaching, was in good part a response to student demands for public accountability and for a voice in governance. (Recall that in the sixties, most industries were facing the issue of consumerism.) In the 1970s, a more gentle use of evaluation was touted—one that was congruent with the older model of higher education. Self-assessment, study, and development were aided by objective information about one's performance. This was a peak period for the growth of campus instructional and faculty development units. In the 1980s, however, management has been faced with a need for objective data in making tough administrative decisions. Naturally enough, the modes of evaluation already on campus (for example, student questionnaire data on teaching) have been pressed into service.

Before directly dealing with Professor Seldin's survey data, allow me to comment briefly on this parody of our history. It should not be taken as a condemnation of recent events. It seems to me that changes in higher education were inevitable, even if unwelcome. Furthermore, a fair observer could present the benefits or the drawbacks of both the earlier and later models. I have attempted to dramatize a change in the campus environment in order to place a consideration of research on evaluation in a human and social context.

The Data. Since we are in that period when evaluation is being taken as a serious activity, it is especially important to learn as much as we can not only about the business of evaluation itself but also about how it is perceived and dealt with on campuses. Professor Seldin's first report provided a baseline against which we can compare data from the later studies. The most recent survey reveals some interesting changes, detailed analysis of which appears elsewhere.

The continued high reported use of student evaluation of teaching is striking. Probably it reflects not only the impact of student demands but also the recognition of competition for the shrinking pool of potential students. We would, of course, like to know more of the kind of evaluation instruments used (for example, campuswide questionnaires) and how the information collected is utilized, a point I will return to below. Heavy reliance upon peer rating of teaching continues as well, a matter of serious discussion among professional evaluators. Balancing this in a sense is the increased attention to research productivity. While public evidence of scholarship is expected to be important in the universities, one would not necessarily predict greater attention to it in the colleges. It seems to me that there is simply a continuation of the trend toward more explicit accountability, with a mixture of focus on the institution (as evidenced by evaluation of teaching, advising, and service) and the discipline (greater stress on research production).

Two additional kinds of information are important when we attempt to construct a comprehensive picture of faculty evaluation: actual use and variability.

Actual use: Academics are, at least in some respects, like other human beings. When they report on their scholarly work, they tend to be constrained by a rugged set of rules. But elsewhere, their verbal behavior responds to the influences that commonly affect all of us. Consequently, reports about variables affecting the evaluation of professors, for example, are as liable to biases and social and political pressures as any other survey data. We need to know how isomorphic these reports are with the actual set of variables that influence decisions on professors' tenure, promotion, and job security. It is no easier to obtain such information than to fathom the inner workings of a jury or the process by which governments arrive at policies. Yet that is the nutmeat that lies inside the shell. Until we crack the shell, we simply will not know the correlation between reported rankings of important variables in decision making and their actual influence.

Going a step further, one should exercise caution in equating ranks with weights. Teaching, research, and service activities almost universally are ranked as of prime importance in determining the value of a faculty member. Professor Seldin's data give us further insight into what specific activities or sources of evidence represent these broad categories. But could we conclude, for example, that although both systematic student and chair evaluation ratings are always used in an evaluation of teaching performance, they affect a decision equally? Probably not. But then what *is* the algebra of the decision-making process? Professor Seldin's work encourages us to seek more detailed answers.

Variability: We know that campuses vary a great deal in

their images. Thus, there are colleges designed for students seeking entrance to graduate studies; some colleges emphasize the sciences, others the humanities, and so on. How do they differ with regard to the methods of faculty evaluation and the actual weightings given to each of the factors ranked high in Professor Seldin's data? I suspect that one outcome of the recent budget tightening and self-examination is that colleges are trying to establish for themselves and for others clearer and more distinct images. A close examination of patterns of evaluation might help us in determining the validity of that hunch. For example, do certain campuses *in fact* emphasize the teaching role of the professor and others require excellence in research? It would be interesting to discover, for instance, that small colleges extremely dependent on student-driven financing are indeed responsive to that pressure and place teaching first among equals when evaluating professors. Does a finer grained analysis of the data reveal a growing dichotomization of colleges into research and teaching campuses?

The Future. What will the face of faculty evaluation in the remainder of this century look like? That is an interesting question, although I think more interesting areas lie below it and are slowly emerging. What will higher education look like, and how will it be evaluated?

Looking at faculty evaluation in the short term, I would predict an unhappy period marked by contention and rancor. At least in some places, colleges and universities will face years more of budget stress. It is likely that faculties will become increasingly militant about job security, promotions, salaries, and the like. Demands will increase for a greater voice in administrative decision making—a recapturing of the faculty prominence in governance. Enmeshed in this will be evaluation (certainly of administrators as well as professors). Unions or approximations thereof will actively examine evaluation procedures. All of this will lead, I hope, to some positive consequences. Colleges and universities will become more sophisticated about evaluation procedures and the interpretation of the information obtained. Professors will reassume a more dynamic role in governance. Types of evaluation will be clearly differentiated, with program evaluation becoming increasingly more important in the next few years. Goals of institutions will become more clearly defined.

And that brings us to the second larger focus: institutional evaluation. About four times as many adult Americans are being taught outside universities and colleges as inside. The differentiation of postsecondary educational institutions (for example, community colleges, correspondence learning institutes, vocational schools) continues to peel branches from the traditional conglomerate tree of the college and university. The increased use of computers as teaching machines and information resources is likely to encourage learning at home or at commercially controlled sites. Applied research activities may or may not be carried out more cost effectively in academic settings than elsewhere. As the cost of conducting basic research increases, support for it, perversely, seems to be diminishing. In short, the traditional activities of colleges and universities, as well as their structures and the roles of their faculties, are being sorely challenged. Which way to turn—if, indeed, turning is the appropriate movement—is a serious question for postsecondary institutions. As financial control of more and more of academia moves into the hands of others, particularly of government, definition of purpose, accountability, and explicit evidence of worth are likely to be demanded by the sponsors.

Evaluation of faculty, then, should be viewed in the larger perspective of the evaluation of the purposes of institutions of higher learning. Will the survival and continued health of the institution be seen as best served by maintaining a professor's primary allegiance to a discipline? Or, consonant with the growth of the industry-like management in postsecondary education, will there be greater demands for loyalty to, service to, and identification with the institution? The potential conflict between the two ("I am a biologist" versus "I work for Mork University") seems to lie in the perception of purposes of the institutions. And these in good part are operationalized in the systems of evaluation. Professor Seldin's continuing descriptions of what is seen as constituting the important components of professoring offer us some glimpses over time of any changes that are occurring in the pattern of valued goals at American colleges.

Evaluation in the Service of Faculty
by Robert J. Menges

As I read the Seldin survey, the following findings about faculty evaluation practices at liberal arts undergraduate colleges seem most important:

- Liberal arts colleges are obviously student oriented. In evaluating overall faculty performance, they place greatest weight on teaching and advising.
- Liberal arts colleges prize service to the campus community, as shown primarily by faculty participation on committees.
- Liberal arts colleges also value seniority, as evidenced by length of service in rank.
- Liberal arts colleges give relatively less weight to research, publication, and work in professional societies, although that weight has been increasing.
- Liberal arts colleges give relatively little weight to personal attributes, and that weight has been decreasing.

Evaluation procedures serve faculty well when they provide decision makers with accurate and varied information in manageable form on all relevant dimensions of faculty work. With this criterion in mind, I shall discuss the survey's three areas: service, scholarship/research, and teaching.

Service. The components of service include work on college and department committees, formal administrative duties, and academic advising. Advising has considerable kinship with teaching, in my view, because it can significantly affect student development. In reality, however, advising more often serves the requirement-meeting needs of students and the record-keeping needs of institutions. Colleges might profitably give greater attention to how the relationships between advising and teaching affect evaluation.

Regarding emphasis on service, the survey shows little

Robert J. Menges is professor at the Center for the Teaching Professions at Northwestern University and coordinator of the School of Education's programs in teaching-learning processes.

change from 1978 to 1983. The quality and quantity of work necessary for "excellence" in service cannot be inferred from the survey, nor do we know how standards may be changing. I suspect that evaluation of service will change less in the future than will evaluation of teaching and of scholarship/research, because comparatively low importance is placed on service.

Scholarship/Research. Regarding scholarship and research, I am intrigued by the types of information most frequently used. According to the survey, greatest emphasis is on published books, articles, monographs, and chapters. That is, emphasis is on scholarly products that have survived appraisal by editors and referees, persons most likely to be at other institutions. Papers presented at meetings where there is prior submission and screening also receive outside review. This evidence from outside sources is then judged by peers and administrators on the home campus.

How do professors in teaching-oriented institutions cope with the increasing emphasis on scholarship? The cynic, assuming that what is important is the *number* of items published, suggests publishing short pieces in high-prestige outlets as quickly as possible. This advice creates practical as well as ethical dilemmas. Is the prestige of a leading journal worth the risk of its high rejection rate and its publication lag? Should the piece be revised for two less prestigious outlets that may more likely accept it and that publish faster, even if they charge for publication? And what of more ambitious projects in progress, such as books? How can manuscripts be assessed when the work is incomplete and time is too short for the screening/publication/review cycle?

This is not a call to de-emphasize scholarship. I firmly believe that scholarly work enriches not only one's teaching but also one's intellectual life and one's value as a colleague. Greater attention to scholarship and research does, however, raise several problems that colleges must address.

1. The laws of conservation of energy, applied to academic life, imply that energy for scholarship is energy taken away from other professional work. Colleges may deal with this problem by becoming more selective in new hires, thereby selecting from today's abundant talent only persons who can do every-

thing well. But what of faculty hired in a different era and with different expectations? Perhaps institutions can support their scholarship by reducing other responsibilities or by bringing groups of faculty together for scholarly activities that complement their teaching or by facilitating research collaborations with students. Other imaginative strategies are needed, always tailored to the liberal arts setting.

2. The proper measure of the value of scholarship is its impact. The cynic's simple measure is publication, but the fact of publication tells us little about diffusion of research findings or about influence of work on others. Information is required about readership and citations and about how the work is reviewed by scholars elsewhere. Yet, according to the survey, citation analysis and peers at other institutions are not widely used in assessing scholarship.

    The impact of nonprint evidence should also be noted, including video or film or performance records of scholarship. Further, we must define appropriate audiences for impact in addition to scholars in one's own specialty. Other potential targets of impact compatible with the liberal arts mission are colleagues in allied disciplines, alumni, student collaborators, and persons who develop instructional materials.

3. Paper-based publication is becoming anachronistic. A world overloaded with information and glutted with the paper holding that information needs alternative means of publication. Well before the year 2000, knowledge dissemination will occur largely independent of paper. Computers will store the work of scholars. Conventions of form, length, and access, even the meaning of *publication* itself, will be redefined. Who declares that publication has occurred? How are the use and impact of scholarly products documented? Indeed, what, when, and where does one find the "product" of research when reports are instantaneously disseminated and revised and disseminated again?

Teaching. Because evaluation of overall performance relies most heavily on teaching, survey results pertaining to teaching deserve scrutiny. First, consider who supplies information and makes judgments about teaching (see Table 9). Participation by department chairs and deans is most frequent (81 percent and 75 percent, respectively). Participation by students is next most frequent (68 percent using systematic ratings and 12 percent using informal opinions). Opinions from alumni and long-term student follow-up are rare (about 4 percent each). Participation by peers occurs at rates of over 40 percent (43 percent for colleague opinions and 46 percent for committees). Self-evaluations are also frequent (42 percent). Since 1978, use of self-evaluations and student ratings has increased, while use of informal student opinions has declined.

Items referring to what is examined show considerably lower frequency. Scholarly research and publication, oddly, is most common (27 percent); classroom visits and syllabi and examinations are next (at 20 percent each, both increasing since 1978). Virtually no attention is paid to students' academic indicators: grade distributions (5 percent), examination performance (4 percent), and enrollment in elective courses (1 percent).

The foregoing analysis seems to imply greater attention to who evaluates than to what is evaluated. The inference is unwarranted, however, since the questionnaire merely lists all items as "sources of information." It is useful to note that for some items, an object is appraised, and that appraisal is subsequently judged by others. For example, a syllabus might be reviewed by peers and their report added to information subsequently considered by a review committee. For other items, an event is observed, and aggregate observations are subsequently judged. For example, classroom behavior is rated by students at the end of a course, and a summary with norms is subsequently considered by the chair.

An evaluation system should make further clarifications, including (1) what is being evaluated—classroom behavior, student projects, examination performance, course materials prepared by the instructor, publications or talks for professional audiences (but only if they are about teaching), and so on; (2) the form in which information is recorded—ratings, narrative reports, checklists, letters, and so on; (3) the level at which information is aggregated—raw data, descriptive summaries, generalizable statements, and so on; (4) the source who reports the information—

students, peers, administrators, alumni, community members, self, and so on; and (5) the source of summative judgments — self, peers, administrators, and so on.

Despite this limitation, the survey reveals some interesting trends. From 1978 to 1983, there was no change in frequency of evaluation by administrators, probably because it was already so high. Use of systematic student ratings has increased, while use of informal student opinions has decreased. There is greater attention to classroom visits, to the syllabus, and to self-evaluation. The four items showing increases represent varied and complementary perspectives on the teaching-learning process, namely, views of the classroom through student eyes, views of the classroom through colleague eyes, views of instruction as represented in course plans, and views of the instructor's intentions and reactions.

Student reports can hardly be ignored, since students have unique opportunities to observe teaching. Further, research shows that student ratings possess satisfactory reliability and validity (Overall and Marsh, 1982). Student evaluations are not substitutes for direct measurement of learning, although ratings do correlate positively with examination performance (Cohen, 1981). It is discouraging that, according to the survey, so little attention is given to examination performance and to grades. The survey also leaves the student's role ambiguous. My view has been that students are reporters of opinions and perceptions rather than judges of performance. Judgments, based in part on student-supplied information, are properly made by others (Menges, 1973).

Colleague reports of classroom visits are poor sources of data, because colleagues neither agree sufficiently on what good teaching is nor observe extensively enough to produce reliable reports (Scriven, 1981). Evaluation based on a sound program of classroom visits is probably prohibitively expensive. A more efficient use of colleagues is to review course materials, including syllabus, assignments, grading procedures, and so on. Neither students nor administrators are as well qualified for that task as colleagues.

The increasing use of self-evaluations (now at 42 percent) is heartening. Teachers under review can hardly be expected to render disinterested judgments, but they can provide otherwise unavailable information, such as intended learning outcomes that are not fully explicated in a syllabus. Further, review committee decisions are better informed if they have access to the teacher's own interpretation of student ratings and other data.

Among teaching evaluation issues important for the future, I shall mention three. First, objections to student participation in evaluation deserve continuing attention. Objections such as "These forms measure mainly popularity" or "Ratings are biased by the teacher's grading policies" or "Course effects are larger than instructor effects" can be countered through research, judicious selection of items, and intelligent use of results. Other objections, such as "Students have no right to evaluate me" or "Student evaluations are a threat to academic freedom" or "Students do not take these forms seriously," rest on assumptions that are not subject to direct empirical test. The assumptions should be deliberated by the academic community even though they are unlikely to lead to consensus.

Second, information about teaching should be varied and credibly presented. Too often, teaching is implicitly defined only as course instruction, and available data are limited to student ratings. Information about nonpresentational aspects of teaching, such as planning, advising, and tutoring, should also be available. (See, for example, the suggestions offered by Shore and others, n.d.) Further, display and interpretation of the information must be deliberately planned. Faculty give differential credibility to computer printouts of student ratings, student written comments, and summaries of student group interviews, and these differences depend in part on the uses perceived for the information. Ory and Braskamp's (1981) conceptual framework — "Who says what, how, to whom, with what effects, and for what purpose?" — poses a considerable research challenge, one that they have begun to answer in a *Guidebook for Evaluating Teaching* (Braskamp and others, 1983). Computer storage and retrieval also affect the amount, type, and accessibility of information. At Northeastern University, professors can call up a display (and subsequent printout) of ratings, request their standing on a variety of norms, and ask for suggestions to improve ratings for items where they feel dissatisfied. The computer delivers all this with speed and confidentiality (Koffman, 1982).

Third, we are on the verge of some radical changes in how people teach and learn and how we think about teaching and learning. Microcomputers, intelligent videodisks, and other products of electronic miniaturization, which underlie the shift from an industrial society to an information society, will transform much of higher education. As true individualized instruction becomes feasible, the need for gathering large groups of students in classrooms will diminish. Intrinsically motivating learning programs will give students individualized feedback, not only on *what* they are learning but also on *how* they learn. Teachers will devote more effort to developing materials and evaluating learning and less effort to presenting course content. The essentially human nature of the teaching enterprise will survive this embrace of technology only if teachers spend more time with individuals or small groups in listening, diagnosing, and coaching and less time in lecturing and explaining. These changes in teaching will require corresponding changes in evaluation. For example, the dimensions of teaching on which evaluation is typically based will likely be modified and weighted differently.

This view of the future requires flexibility in evaluation. Most present evaluation systems, because they are the result of compromise, are inherently conservative. It will be ironic if institutionalized systems inhibit rather than stimulate innovation when something as fundamental as the roles of teacher and learner is in question. Such conservatism serves only the short-term interests of faculty.

In conclusion, the survey reveals or implies some inadequacies in light of the criterion I suggested above, namely, that evaluation procedures serve faculty well when they provide decision makers with accurate and varied information in manageable form on all relevant dimensions of faculty work. In practice, it appears that some relevant dimensions are missing or indistinct. Information should be more varied and could be conveyed more effectively. Although information does seem to be reaching appropriate decision makers, it may take another generation of research to learn precisely how it is used by these judges.

Reflections on Issues Raised by the Commentators

The following discussion had its genesis in the invited commentaries. It highlights similarities and differences in viewpoints and sharpens their thrust. The changes in approaches to faculty rating and research and scholarship, and the effects of these changes in the marketplace and on the measuring of teaching impact are the main areas of concern. The need for changes in faculty rewards is also discussed.

New Rating Game

Several commentators hail the emergence of a new rating game for professors, which is more detailed, systematic, public, and evenhanded than the game it is replacing. Chickering says the changes are "certainly in the right direction," and Arreola perceives "positive fundamental changes in the evaluation process." Eble has some misgivings. He acknowledges as pluses certain changes in the evaluation process: "more identifying of useful data, more care in gathering that data and in using it in informed discussion, and some diffusion of decision-making power." But he laments losing "some of the ease that goes with more casual procedures carried out by someone we trust" and the time-consuming demands of a more exacting and rigorous evaluation process.

Both Eble and Geis point out that changing conditions in higher education are changing faculty evaluation practices. Examples of this point readily come to mind. The systematic ratings so widespread today are clearly the aftermath of the massive influx of student population in the 1960s. Today's greater reliance on research, publication, and discipline-based professional activity coincides with renewed interest in foreign language, mathematics, and English courses that develop writing skills. The close scrutiny of faculty performance and the rigorous discussions preceding promotion/tenure decisions reflect today's academic job market, in which there are more professors than jobs. The nationwide movement to bring solid evidence into the faculty evaluation process is due, at least in part, to the need for evidence that will stand up in court.

Eble and Arreola directly and Chickering indirectly make the connection between more objective, measurable, and substantive data in promotion/tenure decisions and today's flurry of litigation in academia. All the litigation, and even its threat, by professors denied promotion or tenure is forcing institutions to take special pains to find hard data on which to base their decisions. Promotion and tenure must now be made on solid evidence of all significant aspects of a professor's performance, in written form, and in strict adherence to the institution's accepted evaluation procedures.

It would, of course, be the height of naiveté to believe that internal politics and ideological and personality conflicts will henceforth be banished from promotion/tenure decisions. In human affairs, a subjective element so often is furtively present in the decision, and no amount of court surveillance can be expected to uncover it. But the courts have had a generally chilling effect on the built-in discriminatory practices of many faculty evaluation systems. For that alone academia is obligated to the courts.

Research/Scholarship

One of the study's findings is that research/scholarship is in growing favor in the evaluation of classroom teaching performance. It touched off strong reactions by Aleomoni, Arreola, Aubrecht, and Menges on the tug-of-war between research and teaching. They should be read carefully. In this writer's view, research and publication play a vital role, particularly in institutions that make them part of the college's stated mission. But a professor's research and publication are often indistinctly related to classroom teaching. Few professors discuss their research in the classroom. The research may even be at odds with the professor's teaching responsibilies. How?

First, the hours devoted to research may be hours borrowed from teaching preparation. Second, the kind of satisfaction associated with research and publication, which will be read by hundreds or thousands of one's peers, is of a different order from the satisfaction associated with the mind expansion in a classroom of nineteen- and twenty-year-olds. Third, the reward system at most colleges and universities today favors research and publication, so a professor who dedicates his full energy to classroom teaching may find his job in jeopardy. With a publish-or-perish sword overhead, the professor who fervently wishes to be an excellent teacher faces a dilemma. He or she must devote a large block of time to both teaching and research. Fourth, teachers and researchers may be opposite personality types. Eble (1976, p. 19) observes that one type "likes to work alone, responds poorly to outside distractions and pressures, is more at ease with the stuff of ideas, facts, and materials of a discipline than with students and learning." The other type "seeks out company, can handle pressures and distractions, and prefers interacting with students to manipulating materials or ideas."

Thus, if it is true that research is often indistinctly related to classroom teaching, then using research as a measure of teaching effectiveness, as is increasingly the practice today, is of grave concern. This is hardly to argue, of course, that research and publication are unimportant. On the contrary, research and publication are two essential but different activities, and it is no sounder to judge professors' classroom teaching performance from their research and publication records than to judge their research and publication records from their classroom teaching performance.

Curiously, many faculty members harbor anxieties and hostility for an evaluation of their teaching on the basis of classroom performance. Why do so many embrace research and publication as somehow a more appropriate measure of faculty performance? Eble (1982) suggests several reasons. First, research by its nature is detached from the individual, and though it hurts personally to have a journal article rejected, the hurt is not as personal as the criticism of one's teaching. Second, most research is assessed at a distance from one's colleagues. The decision to accept or reject a manuscript is made by anonymous reviewers, not by department colleagues. Those who make adverse decisions may have done so from bad motives, but they are not supposed friends and colleagues. Third, teaching has no quantitative measure as definite, for example, as the counting of publications. And as inappropriate as that measure is, it is a tangible means of separating those who have written more from those who have written less.

Fortunately, during the past decade an increasing number of faculty members have accepted, possibly grudgingly, an appraisal of teaching performance based on systematic student evaluations, classroom observations, and reviews of teaching materials. As McKeachie (1967, p. 211) observes: "It is the very complexity of the teaching situation that makes every bit of empirical information the more precious."

Impact of Changes in the Workplace

Faculty evaluation practices in colleges and universities are also undergoing change due to student enrollment shifts, which, in turn, are due to the changing workplace. This issue is addressed by Chickering. Departments and programs wax and wane in accordance with student enrollment. Today, for example, colleges of education are shrinking on virtually every campus, as colleges of business are expanding. Inevitably, then, many institutions find a surplus of faculty members, many of whom are tenured, in the college of education and a shortage of faculty members in the college of business. The answer for many institutions is the retraining and reassignment of some professors.

At that point, the faculty evaluation practices are critical, because the appraisal may possibly turn up business experience or, at least, an interest in teaching business subjects. If so, the institution can retain tried and proven personnel and shift the professors to areas in dire need of teachers. To attain this dual benefit, institutions have to maintain a continuously updated inventory of evaluative data plus the backgrounds and interests of all faculty members. A number of institutions are now doing this. At the University of Hartford (Connecticut), for example, ten professors who had only a passing acquaintance with computers enrolled in a crash summer course. By September, they were teaching beginner courses at Hartford's Computer Center. Previously, they had taught courses ranging from political science to music.

Impact of Computers

Today, there is a nationwide shortage of qualified computer instructors, many of whom have been lured away by higher salaries in business. Despite tight budgets, colleges and universities have had to come up with competitive salaries to attract instructors for computer courses, which are multiplying like rabbits (see Aubrecht's commentary). Some institutions have raised the ante; others have balked, preferring to retrain and reassign faculty members who are redundant in other departments; some are using both methods.

Students are not alone in believing they have a vital stake in the unfolding computer age. Many educators believe that computers are destined to have a major impact on the way teaching and learning will take place in the future classroom. If so, computers will also have major impact on institutional evaluations of faculty performance (see the commentaries by Geis and Menges). Already the computers have penetrated college courses in sociology and education, where they are used to gather information from other disciplines; in English, where they are used for word processing; in business, where they are used for simulation and model building.

Electronic miniaturization is beginning to transform the traditional teaching-learning mode in higher education. Professors who use computers and intelligent videodisks in their classes are destined to alter their teaching methods. They will spend more time in individual coaching and small-group instruction and less time lecturing in auditoriums filled with students. Computers are beginning to affect many faculty evaluation programs. At Northeastern University (Massachusetts), for example, professors can obtain a computer printout that includes their student ratings, their standing on a variety of norms, and specific recommendations to strengthen areas requiring improvement.

Seasoned observers in higher education do not foresee computers replacing the traditional teaching methods of all professors. Many will continue to use large-class lecture and discussion methods of use them well. The future probably holds a mixture of the traditional and new, which will open more teaching options for professors and learning options for students.

Algebra of Faculty Evaluation

Among the first acquisitions of most newly hired faculty members is a copy of the faculty handbook, which contains factual information on the institution's promotion and tenure practices. In general, the handbook makes broad reference to the importance of demonstrated competence in teaching, research, and service. The handbook is rare that offers specific weighting of the three factors, and should a new professor ask for such algebra, the response will depend on who is asked the question. If it is an administrator, the response will most likely be that all three factors are important. Excellence in teaching, the administrator is likely to add, is also rewarded by promotion and tenure. If it is a faculty member, the response will most likely be that promotion and tenure are awarded to those who do considerable research and publishing. Teaching, he or she is likely to add, is unrewarded. The gap between what institutions say and what they do is measured in the commentaries of Aleomoni, Chickering, Geis, and Eble, which deserve an attentive reading.

Who would want to argue that the specifics of what is expected of professors should be kept from them? Yet, in fact, all too many professors have only a vague awareness of what constitutes exemplary, even satisfactory performance. To close the gap between theory and practice, it is urged that the professor meet with the department chairperson at the start of the academic year, and the two of them should hammer out a specific agreement on the weighting of the criteria to be used in the professor's evaluation. The agreement should be consonant with the institution's and the department's needs. It should also spell out in specific terms how the professor's performance standards will be measured at the end of the academic year.

During the year, should the professor be perceived by the department chairperson as failing in serious respects to meet the performance standards, the failure should be discussed with the professor. The discussion should be frank, factual, and far in advance of any promotion/tenure decision. The professor should be given a genuine opportunity to cure the failure and to grow in ways mutually acceptable to the professor and the institution. He or she should be encouraged to participate in faculty development activities such as workshops and microteaching and given the opportunity to consult sympathetic and knowledgeable colleagues on teaching methods, handling difficult students, test construction, and other problems as they arise.

Measuring the Impact of Professors

Some educators still believe that the professors' publishing records provide the best measure of their research/scholarship performance. Others still believe that how much and how well students learn is the cardinal sign of teaching effectiveness. The commentaries of Chickering and Menges address the fallacies in these beliefs.

Research/Scholarship. The best that can be said for an appraisal of research/scholarship based on a publication count is that it is hazardous. Some professors write ten articles while others rewrite the same article ten times. Some professors churn out lightweight articles while others spend years on one seminal monograph. What does productivity in terms of numbers really mean, or what should it mean, to colleagues, administrators, legislators?

Even counting only refereed journals as bona fide publications falls short, because many excellent journals are not refereed. And referees are known to reject a manuscript not because of dubious scholarship but because of philosophical viewpoint. Publications have differing editorial policies favoring short articles, long ones, experimentally based articles, philosophical ones. Academic justice demands that the article and the journal be judged, rather than the journal's refereed or nonrefereed status.

How is the impact of a professor's research/scholarship to be determined? By looking hard for clues indicating the influence of the work on others. One clue is citations by other professors. Another is a flurry of letters to journal editors reacting for or against a work. Still another is the stimulation of more research by others, either replicating the work or expanding its boundaries.

Teaching. Trying to measure the impact of teaching by

quantifying student learning is a highly questionable procedure. It is possible, for example, that modest learning by average students reflects teaching prowess superior to stunning learning by superior students. How does a 20-point student gain in an average class compare with a 30-point student gain in a gifted class? Or a 40-point gain in a remedial class? Student learning is sometimes only the indirect result of teaching. At the end of an intensive honors management seminar in advanced motivation theory, for example, some students may be invited to present papers at a prestigious industrial conference. Without doubt, the teacher deserves credit. But how much credit? How much is due to the gifted students themselves? How much to the institution for developing the special program and admitting only the top students? In short, how is something that is inherently indivisible to be divided among professor, student, and institution? Only a latter-day Solomon can decide. No doubt, student achievement is influenced by an effective professor. But the professor is hardly the only influence. The quantity and quality of student learning are also affected by the student's general academic ability, motivation to learn, organizing and writing ability on exams, skill in multiple-choice exams, study habits, and image, favorable or unfavorable, in the professor's mind. Each factor affects student achievement.

Even when students in two sections of the same course are taught by two professors, it would be improper to use student achievement as a measure of teaching effectiveness. There is a relatively uniform achievement level of students across the board. A study of final examinations indicates that students often learn similar amounts from different professors. In a reanalysis of data from nearly 100 comparative studies of college teaching, Dubin and Taveggia (1968) document the lack of achievement differences. McKeachie (1981) speculates that when the same textbook is used in a multiple-section course, achievement differences tend to be submerged by the textbook, regardless of differences in teaching methods and skills. The bottom line is that it is virtually impossible to isolate teaching and learning. As Eble (1972, p. 63) observes: "Within the institutional context, the forces that bear upon a student's learning in any class are probably as wide as his range of activities and thoughts during the quarter."

Need for a Revised Faculty Reward Structure

It is no exaggeration to say that the most critical problem confronted in the social organization of any (college or) university is
the proper evaluation of faculty services, and giving due recognition through impartial assignment of status. — *Logan Wilson*

More than forty years ago, Logan Wilson made that statement in *The Academic Man* (1942). The need for improved faculty
evaluation and reward systems still exists today. If anything, the
need is increasing exponentially in institutions of higher education as enrollment declines, faculty is surplus, costs are climbing,
and litigation cases multiply. Troubled by these problems,
Aleomoni, Aubrecht, and Eble discuss the vital importance today
of flexibility and individualization of the academic reward system.

Generalities about effective teaching and productive scholarship need nailing down to the professor's day-to-day activities
and priorities and the department's and institution's pressing
needs. One answer is the "faculty growth contract," where the
department chairperson and the professor arrange an agreement
in specific terms of the professor's proposed achievements in a
stipulated time. The evaluation of the professor's performance is
then confined to an appraisal of the proposed and actual accomplishments. The rationale is that each professor's evaluation needs
to be individualized and judged accordingly. A twenty-six-year-old
assistant professor's performance cannot be expected to be the same
as a sixty-year-old full professor's. Each faculty member contributes
differently, and each merits personal discussion and the fixing of performance expectations with the department chairperson.

The Present Reward System. Today, on campuses across
the nation, the sacred cows continue to be research and publication. Teaching, to a large extent, is benignly neglected. Yet this
neglect is certainly not due to lack of interest by faculty members.
Rather, it can be traced to factors quietly pervading the institutions of higher education, which include (1) lack of teaching preparation during graduate education, (2) insufficient in-service
education compared to that found in other professions, and (3)
inadequate promotion-and-tenure policies to support and reward

teaching. Many faculty members believe that teaching merits higher value in institutional reward systems. The loudest criticism against the current reward system is that teaching is pitted against research, and teaching becomes the automatic loser because of the high visibility of research. Teaching is largely a private affair between the professor and students behind a closed classroom door. The results of research are published and become a matter of public discussion. No wonder institutions of higher education place higher store on research and fail to reward even outstanding teaching performance. Aleomoni and Arreola express disquiet on this point in their commentaries.

As a result of the emphasis on research, the outstanding teacher is often regarded in the department no differently from the mediocre teacher. Indeed, the latter can hide classroom mediocrity behind glittering research. There is some truth in the wry notion that a professor is paid to teach but is evaluated and rewarded for research and publication. This situation has developed partly because of the venerable belief that the college professor must be not simply a teacher but a scholar who pushes back the frontiers of knowledge in the discipline. The belief gains credence by the insistence of some academics that teaching performance simply does not lend itself to evaluation. Good teaching defies definition. It is so singular, they say, that it is incapable of measurement. Actually, teaching can be assessed as rigorously as research and publication and has been for years by many institutions. Student ratings, classroom visits, colleague reviews of teaching materials, alumni opinions, self-assessments, and special incidents have been systematically gathered and judiciously interpreted at many institutions. The three-dimensional professor emerges. The process has flaws, but it is reasonably workable and will serve until it is further improved.

Rewarding Teaching. What is clearly needed today in the academic reward system is greater recognition of superior teaching. It should take its rightful place beside research and publication. Excellent teaching requires scholarly demands equally as great as but of a different order than research and publication. The same high level of conceptual and analytical thinking, the time, energy, and personal dedication that characterize research and publication also characterize superior teaching. Because of special interest, temperament, and inclination, some faculty members favor one or the other. But this is often a matter of degree rather than exclusion. And it may shift from time to time. As Eble (1972, p. 28) states: "A minimum faculty reward system should lead faculty members to devote their energies to one at some periods and to the other at other times. The system should give all members of the faculty the opportunity and incentive to develop both as teachers and as men and women of knowledge." This is a call for belated recognition of first-rate teaching in the reward system. It is a call for twin recognition of research/publication and good teaching.

The route to promotion and tenure should as easily be traversed by effective teaching as by scholarly research. There is room and need for both in institutions of higher education. Both also have to be periodically evaluated. That brings up once again faculty evaluation methods. And caution is in order.

Although faculty evaluation is more art than science and is practiced by fallible human beings, much has been learned in recent years about what works and what fails. Today, the faculty evaluation process commands center stage for reasons already described at length. Some institutions may shortsightedly try to paper over the holes in their evaluation structures. But this cosmetic approach does not address the hard-core issues and is doomed to failure. Other, more farsighted institutions will take a longer view. They will acknowledge weaknesses in their faculty evaluation systems and will devote the necessary time, energy, and resources to dismantle and rebuild them. Their goal will be construction of a new system that is at once flexible, comprehensive, objective, individualized, fair, and consistent with the law. These institutions will view the intense pressures on higher education today not as roadblocks but rather as stepping-stones.

Chapter 5

Building Successful Evaluation Programs:

Improving Faculty Performance, Tenure Decisions, and the Promotion Process

In recent years, many hundreds of research studies and position papers on faculty evaluation have been published. Comprehensive analyses and summaries of the literature by Centra (1979), Seldin (1980), Millman (1981), and Braskamp and others (1983) have appeared. This chapter makes abundant use of research findings but is based primarily on more than a decade of the writer's experience in assisting hundreds of colleges and universities to develop successful faculty evaluation programs. The chapter's focus is practical rather than theoretical. It offers pragmatic advice on what seems to work effectively and what does not.

The cornerstone of every faculty evaluation program is its purpose: the purpose influences the kind of questions asked, sources of data, depth of data analysis, and dissemination of findings. In institutions of higher education today, the two leading purposes for faculty evaluation are to improve performance and to provide the rationale for administrative decisions on tenure, promotion in rank, and retention.

Evaluation to Improve Performance

There is no greater purpose for performance evaluation than to improve the performance. That is achieved by using the evaluation to assist the faltering, to encourage the tired, and to direct the indecisive. Professors are hired, promoted, and granted tenure by colleges and universities in expectation of first-class performance. To evaluate professors to improve their performance is no more than a logical extension of this expectation and provides practical evidence of administrative good faith. Just as students need guidance to correct errors, professors are entitled to helpful direction to improve performance. *Dissonance* is the modish word used to describe the most compelling reason for a teacher to wish to improve performance. Feedback from constructive performance evaluation will often set up in the professor the kind of dissonance, or dissatisfaction, that acts as the psychological spur to improvement.

Does evaluation really result in better performance? It depends. Better performance is more likely if (1) the appraisal results are new to the professor, (2) the professor is motivated to improve, and (3) the professor knows how to bring about the improvement. One fact is clear. Simply to turn over the evaluation results to the teacher is probably predestined to lead nowhere. What is far more likely to trigger improved performance is a discussion of the evaluation results with a sympathetic and knowledgeable colleague or a teaching-improvement specialist. The teacher needs reassurance that the shortcomings are neither unusual nor insurmountable and wise counsel on how to overcome them.

If evaluative feedback is to be converted into teaching improvement, it must be derived from multiple sources: classroom observation, student evaluation, self-appraisal, samples of instructional material, a videotaped classroom session. The data must be detailed and diagnostic in nature. They must spotlight particular teaching behaviors (is the professor fair and impartial in dealing with students?) and course characteristics (is the assigned reading too difficult?). The probing questions would, of course, appear as items on a scale rather than call for a yes or no response, which would not yield the kind of specificity required for performance improvement. It is preferable to issue rating forms to students, colleagues, and the professor to be appraised and to videotape a classroom session early in the term rather than at the end. About five weeks into the term is suggested. With the ratings and videotape in hand, the professor's performance can thereafter be monitored and deficiencies corrected.

Performance evaluation need not be restricted to the classroom. It is equally applicable to the professor's role as student adviser or as a scholar engaged in research and publication. The process is the same. It includes gathering detailed data from a range of sources, joint analysis of the data by the professor and an esteemed faculty colleague or consultant, isolating and identifying the skills requiring improvement, and planning and implementing the corrective action. The confidentiality of the data must at all costs remain inviolate. If data are shared, it must be with the consent and at the discretion of the appraised professor. For data surreptitiously to be used for personnel decisions would have an immediately chilling, even fatal, effect on the credibility of the entire evaluation program.

In an ideal world, faculty evalutions would be conducted separately for the purposes of improving teaching (formative) and making personnel decisions (summative), since one may have great impact on the other. But because of vital time and financial constraints, many institutions find that they cannot conduct the two evaluations separately. Instead, they conduct them simultaneously by integrating into a single questionnaire both the core items useful to administrators in personnel decisions and selected items useful to the faculty member to improve performance. Who receives which feedback? Instructors are given their rating results on all questions, but administrators are given results only of the core items.

Evaluation for Personnel Decisions

Professorial assessment also provides a rational, objective, and equitable basis for critical administrative decisions on tenure, promotion in rank, and retention. These decisions have always been made by colleges and universities, but fiscal and other pressures in recent years have moved personnel decisions to the number one reason for evaluation for many institutions.

Standards for tenure are more rigorous today. Granting tenure can commit an institution to a salary plus benefits exceeding $700,000 over a thirty-year period. As a result, some colleges and universities even impose percentage limits on tenured faculty within the institution and within the department. Standards for promotion in rank are also tougher. Many institutions set tight limits on the number of promotions for each academic rank. At one institution, forty-five assistant professors competed for the four associate professor positions allocated by the institution for 1983–84. Confronted by difficult personnel decisions, many institutions are demanding harder evidence of academic achievement. Not infrequently, institutions bring in outside reviewers for third-party appraisals of a professor's publication record and other contributions.

As an aid to administrative decisions, virtually every college and university has constructed some sort of faculty evaluation system. Unfortunately, in the heady rush to judgments, some of the patchwork constructions relied on faulty data-gathering methods and poorly devised rating instruments. The result was as predictable as it was unfortunate. In constructing a system to evaluate faculty for personnel decisions, the following benchmarks must be observed:

1.   There must be a clear linkage between academic rewards and the evaluation program. If the process produces only negative consequences, it is inviting failure. What good is a system that produces faculty resentment and discredits itself?

2.   All professors must be familiar with the performance standards by which they will be evaluated. And they must know specifically what constitutes satisfactory and exemplary performance. Professors who fail significantly to meet the standards must have their shortcomings discussed in detail far in advance of major personnel decisions. They should be encouraged and shown how to overcome the shortcomings.

3.   A clear description, point by point, of the entire evaluation program should be communicated in writing as soon as

possible. Professors must know the specific criteria underpinning administrative decisions, together with their responsibilities in providing dossier materials and the responsibilities of administrators in evaluating professorial performance.

4. The evaluation program, section by section, must be openly and democratically arrived at, in the full light of publicity. Open hearings and faculty forums are particularly useful. Gentle persuasion and human understanding instead of strident voices and debating points should characterize the hearings and forums. The faculty must have a significant hand in both developing and running the evaluation program. The faculty must be aware of its key role and always feel it is in full control of its own destiny.

5. The evaluation policies and practices must have the active support of top-level academic administrators. They must be publicly committed to the program and see that it operates effectively. They must provide whatever resources are necessary to the program.

6. The evaluation policies and practices must be in accordance with established civil rights guidelines. In recent years, it is the lucky institution that escapes lawsuits by aggrieved professors who believe they have been denied tenure, promotion, or contract renewal for discriminatory reasons. Evaluation programs in increasing numbers are being challenged in court as inadequate or biased. And a mounting number of institutions have been judged in violation of affirmative action clauses and civil rights laws and ordered by the courts to reverse personnel decisions. It is critically important, therefore, for institutions to shore up inadequacies and erase inequities in their faculty evaluation programs before the courts order the changes.

7. The program should take into account the tendency that professors share with most human beings to regard evaluation as an implicit threat. This natural resistance must be nullified by genuine understanding and by adding up the numerous advantages to professors of objective, fact-based administrative personnel decisions. It is a much more effective approach than to flex administrative muscle, which, instead of ending faculty resistance, simply drives it underground. To soften faculty resistance, experience suggests that sufficient time — a year or even two years —

should be allowed for acceptance and implementation, the evaluation system should be viewed as experimental and not as etched
in stone, and dry runs should be conducted to gain experience
and to locate and correct program weaknesses.

8.   Starting from zero to develop a faculty evaluation program to reinvent the wheel. Many programs operate with success around the country. An institution desiring a program would
be prudent to adapt, not adopt, an existing program by tailoring
it to meet local needs, politics, traditions.

9.   To obtain a three-dimensional and reasonably accurate
picture of a professor's effectiveness, a number of relevant sources
must be consulted (Seldin, 1981). Each information source offers
important but limited insight. No single source is enough for tenure, promotion, and retention decisions. All of them together
build a more solid foundation for administrative decisions. *Students*
provide an assessment of teaching skills, content and structure of
the course, work load, teacher-student interactions, organization
of course materials and clarity of presentation, and student advising. *Faculty peers* provide a review of teaching materials (assignments, handouts, tests, papers), mastery and currency of subject
matter, original research, professional recognition, participation
in the academic community, interest in and concern for teaching, and service to the nonacademic community. *Administrators*
provide an appraisal of the work load and other teaching responsibilities, student course enrollment, service to the institution,
and teaching improvement. The professor provides self-appraisal
as a teacher (and as a faculty member with added academic accomplishments, student advising, committee memberships, and service to the institution and community. Experience suggests that
in addition to multiple sources, successful evaluation programs
also use multiple methods to obtain information on faculty performance. Among the more popular methods are ratings and surveys,
individual and group interviews, classroom observation and videotaping, written appraisals of service, and research/scholarship
contributions by on- and off-campus personnel. In practice, the
number of methods is limited by time, cost, and magnitude of
the decision.

10. The evaluation instruments and procedures must provide reliable and valid data that are comparable within academic units. The data must be of proper technical level and quality to be trustworthy and used exclusively for the purported purpose.

11. Several review levels and a clearly defined appeals process must be built into the program. These procedural safeguards will detect errors of fact and interpretation and instill confidence in the integrity of the program.

Evaluating Teaching Performance

Some professors st'll argue that teaching cannot be evaluated because no one knows even how to define effective teaching. And they automatically downgrade the growing number of scholarly investigations that are sorting out effective and ineffective teaching behaviors. Undoubtedly, it is true that many pieces to the teaching-learning puzzle are still missing. But today the nature of effective teaching is more precisely known than the more elusive definitions of beauty, love, good taste. More often, when professors argue that teaching cannot be evaluated, they mean that teaching should not be evaluated. Or they are expressing their concerns about how and by whom it should be evaluated.

The hallmarks of good teaching are reasonably consistent in most studies. They include being well prepared for class, demonstrating comprehensive subject knowledge, motivating students, being fair and reasonable in managing the details of learning, and being sincerely interested in the subject matter and in teaching itself. How can the presence or absence of these qualities in a professor be known? Students, faculty colleagues, and the teachers themselves each play a key role in the collective evaluation of teaching performance.

Student Evaluation

Theoretically, student opinion of a professor includes an exit interview, suggestion box, small discussion group, alumni questionnaire, face-to-face discussion, and student testimonial. In practice, a written questionnaire or rating scale generally serves as the foremost source of administrative information. Will the use of student ratings automatically lead to improved teaching? For most professors, probably not. In fact, low ratings and critical student comments can easily lead to anxiety, discouragement, and loss of teaching enthusiasm. Student ratings are more likely to produce a salutary effect when followed by faculty counseling that encourages and suggests other teaching strategies.

Since student ratings are easy to administer and score, they are in popular use today for personnel decisions. Unfortunately, they are also widely abused. There can be no doubt that student ratings are an important element in evaluating teaching performance. But this does not mean that student ratings by themselves are sufficient evidence of teaching effectiveness. Student ratings are only part of the whole. Proper weight must be given to other sources. Students are an excellent source, for example, on the degree of intellectual curiosity and interest in the subject stimulated by the teacher in the classroom. But faculty peers are certainly more competent judges of the scholarly content of the course and the professor's mastery of the subject. In short, students provide useful appraisals of both course and instructor, provided the questions they are asked are appropriate to students.

Reliability and Validity. Are student ratings reliable? Valid? Hundreds of researchers have probed these questions in the past decade (for comprehensive reviews of the literature, see McKeachie, 1979, and Braskamp and others, 1983).

The test of reliability means that the same result is yielded no matter how often or where the test is performed. In the matter of student ratings, virtually every study measuring their reliability has reported a high level of stability and consistency. Validity means that the instrument measures what it is supposed to measure. The key to the validity of student ratings is whether the instructors rated effective by students are generally those whose students achieve most. Although study results are not uniform, McKeachie (1979, p. 390) concludes that student ratings are "highly valid as indices of achievement of attitudinal and motivational goals of education and are reasonably valid as indices of achievement of cognitive goals." Braskamp and others (1983, p. 15), on the basis of a review of the literature, also conclude that student ratings are valid: "they have sufficient validity to warrant their use for both personnel decisions and improvement purposes."

Are Student Ratings Influenced by Other Factors? In general, most factors that might be expected to influence student ratings have relatively small or no effect.

Student Characteristics. Age, sex, student level, and personality have scant effect on student ratings. The single most important variable affecting satisfaction is probably student expectation. Students who expect a teacher to be good generally find the teacher measuring up to that expectation. In part, the reason may be that these students are more attentive, motivated, and disposed to learn than students who enter the classroom with low expectation.

Course and Class Characteristics. Size of class, subject matter, and whether the class is required or elective may affect ratings to a small degree. In general, slightly higher ratings are awarded to professors who teach courses that have fewer than fifteen students, that are required, and that are in the behavioral or social sciences. It is only prudent, therefore, to avoid placing heavy weight on comparisons of the ratings of professors teaching courses differing greatly in such characteristics.

Instructor Characteristics. Sex, professional rank, and grading standards (assuming they are within the range of normal variability) have minimal effect on student ratings. Is there a relationship between student ratings and instructor personality? Most researchers conclude that the instructors who garner the highest ratings are "substance" teachers, not merely entertainers. Professors who display energy, humor, and enthusiasm and are content oriented tend to be rated highly by students. Since they turn out to be the same professors who arouse student interest in subject matter and, consequently, more student learning, it is appropriate that they receive the laurels from their students.

Cautions. Unfortunately, the potential value of student ratings is often negated by misuse or abuse. Experience suggests the following:

1. Don't use the ratings from a single class as the springboard for tenure or promotion decisions. Cumulative ratings over several years and from a range of courses are the proper index.

2. Don't use the ratings as the only source of information on teaching performance. Use classroom observation, self-evaluation, review of course materials, and trained evaluators and assessors of student learning, among other sources.

3. Don't misinterpret small differences between mean scores. A professor who receives a mean rating of 3.78 on a 4-point scale is not a significantly better teacher than a colleague who receives a mean rating of 3.75.

4. Develop and adhere to fixed guidelines on how the ratings will be used. Evaluation obtained to help improve instruction must not become part of the instructor's personnel file.

5. Standardize the administration of the ratings. Tell the students how their ratings will be used and have a student assistant read a statement of instructions to the class. The instructor must be out of the room during this process. The completed forms should be sealed in the presence of the students and immediately taken to a secured location. They should be processed within two weeks but the results not given to instructors until after final grades are issued.

6. It is not worth having student evaluations if they generate a level of anxiety, conflict, confusion, or anger that adversely affects the administration of education.

Choosing an Instrument for Student Ratings. Colleges and universities have ready access to the experience and rating instruments developed at other institutions of higher education. It is not difficult to adapt an instrument to fit local needs, since most rating scales contain both a surplus of items and blank spaces for the insertion of additional items (see Exhibits 1, 2, and 3). The questionnaire's length and the selection of items depend on the purpose. For faculty members desiring improved classroom performance, a medium (sixteen to twenty items) or long form (thirty to thirty-six items) is appropriate. Diagnostic questions that ask for perceptions or evaluations of specific teaching behaviors or specific aspects of the course are likely to be more helpful than general questions. In constructing a scale, include several items (similar to the sample item) from each of the following groupings:

1. Impact on students. ("My intellectual curiosity has been stimulated by this instructor.")
2. Rapport. ("The instructor is friendly.")
3. Group interaction. ("Students discuss one another's ideas.")
4. Work load. ("The instructor asks for too much work.")
5. Structure. ("The instructor plans class activities in detail.")
6. Feedback. ("Tests and papers and graded and returned promptly.")

For the improvement of classroom performance, several open-end questions should be included to allow students to respond in their own words. ("List the three traits you liked most about the instructor.")

If student ratings are to be used for personnel decisions, a short form (four to six items) normally suffices. The items should be carefully phrased to be valid for all courses and indifferent to instructional style. Since comparisons of instructors in different courses are shaky at best, it is prudent not to attempt much more than to determine whether students rate an instructor as excellent, good, fair, or poor. One question on how much the instructor stimulated interest and curiosity and another question or two on overall effectiveness should be enough. Experience urges the following key considerations when using student ratings for personnel decisions:

1. A minimum of 75 percent of the registered students in a class must complete the rating form to assure credibility of the results.
2. Ratings in several courses over several semesters are required for a reasonably accurate presentation of student views. Even then, they need careful interpretation by peers or administrators in a position to know.
3. Global or overall ratings are more appropriate than diagnostic ratings of specific teaching behaviors.
4. Summing ratings on a group of questions to compute a mean assumes that the items measure the same thing—effective teaching. Most scales contain several types of questions for different purposes, which cannot meaningfully be combined.

5. Rating forms must be administered, collected, and tallied systematically.

6. Instructors often have no idea how their ratings compare with their peers'. Some institutions have solved the problem by issuing an interpretation manual containing norms (average scores, percentiles, and so on) to make comparisons possible. The normative comparison should be compatible with the specific characteristics of a teacher and course (for example, small, advanced honors seminar).

7. The survey forms should be distributed during the last two weeks of the semester, but the period immediately before or during final exams should be avoided.

8. Faculty members should be extended the right to participate in the selection of items or forms for use in evaluating teaching. This will help assure that the items or forms are appropriate to the goals of the particular class. Some institutions and departments utilize a set of core questions that appear on all rating forms and add items selected by the instructor from an extensive catalogue listing.

9. Enough space should be allowed on rating forms for comments. Students need the opportunity to express thoughts that may not fit the questionnaire format. Comments may provide clues that clarify the underlying reason for the rating or point to needed teaching changes.

10. "Evaluation fatigue" may set in if student ratings are required in every course every semester. Many institutions skirt the problem by calling for ratings every second or third semester.

11. When ratings are used for personnel decisions, faculty members should be afforded the opportunity to examine and offer an interpretation of the data or introduce additional relevant evidence.

Students cannot and must not be asked to pass judgments on the professor's mastery of the subject, the appropriateness of instructional objectives or reading lists, or the currency of course materials. These judgments are best left to the professor's colleagues.

To sum up, student ratings are necessary but not sufficient

by themselves to appraise teaching performance. Additional information from other sources is required for a reasonably sound final judgment. For personnel decisions, more sources of information are particularly pertinent.

Colleague Evaluation

Faculty members seem generally agreed that student ratings are inadequate to judge the whole professor. Most professors also consider a formal system of appraisal better than an informal one. Nonetheless, there is a strong pocket of resistance among professors to add colleague ratings to the appraisal system. Some argue that colleague ratings demand excess faculty time and effort. Others say that to speak their minds about their colleagues' performance is awkward and even a bit hazardous to their own professional futures. And still others make the point that educational goals are best achieved in an academic atmosphere of cooperation and mutual respect. To make evaluative judgments of each other, they argue, would pollute the academic atmosphere with suspicions and anxieties.

Granting some merit to these arguments, the issue must be balanced by the inherent benefit in expanding the evaluative base. If it is accepted that faculty evaluation deserves serious attention on every college and university campus, are not colleagues in a unique position to offer sound judgment on a professor's performance? Today, colleague evaluations are integral to systems that are operating successfully in many institutions of higher education. Actually, to exclude colleague evaluations because of anxiety over possible retaliations or other repercussions demeans the academic profession.

In evaluating teaching effectiveness, which criteria are colleagues in an especially advantageous position to judge? Experience suggests the following areas: (1) selection and mastery of course content; (2) appropriateness of course objectives and instructional materials; (3) appropriate methodology for teaching specified sections of courses; (4) appropriate techniques to foster and measure student learning; (5) course organization; (6) student achievement based on exams, projects, presentations, and reports; (7) concern for and interest in teaching; and (8) homework assignments, textbooks, and handouts. The two clear windows to a professor's classroom performance and examination of instructional materials and classroom visitations.

Examination of Instructional Materials. A detailed examination of instructional materials would include the following items:

Course Content. Is it up to date? Is the instructor's treatment fair and lively? Are conflicting views presented? Are the breadth and depth of coverage appropriate for the course? Has the instructor mastered the subject matter?

Course Objectives. Have the objectives been clearly communicated to the students? Are they consistent with the department's overall objectives? If the course is a building block for a more advanced course, are the students being properly prepared?

Methodology. Are the instructor's learning approaches (lectures, discussion, films, fieldwork, outside speakers) suitable to the course objectives? Is the pacing varied? Do students use the library for the course? Would audiovisual or television services strengthen the course?

Grading and Examinations. Is the examination suitable to content and course objectives? Are tests graded and returned promptly? Are the grading standards understood by students? Is the grade distribution pattern appropriate for the course level?

Course Organization. Is the syllabus current and relevant to the course outline? Are the outline and topic sequence logical? Is the difficulty level appropriate for the course level?

Student Achievement. How do students perform in more advanced courses? Do students apply in their papers and projects the principles learned in the course? What is the general quality of major homework assignments?

Interest in Teaching. Does the instructor discuss teaching with colleagues? Seek advice on teaching from others? Participate in discussions and committees devoted to teaching? Publish on teaching-related issues? Is the instructor sought by colleagues for advice? Knowledgeable about current developments in teaching the discipline?

Homework Assignments. Do homework assignments supplement lectures and class discussions? Do assignments reflect appropriate course goals? Is the reading list relevant to course and department goals? Is it appropriate to the course level?

Although peers are in an advantageous position to systematically evaluate a colleague's instructional materials, few do so. In part, the reason is that most institutions have not integrated this function into their evaluative systems. In institutions that have, a procedure that has proved successful opens with the instructor providing a faculty committee with course syllabi, reading lists, instructional handouts, copies of examinations, and homework assignments. The instructor completes a standard form on course objectives and instructional methods used. Faculty committee members familiar with the subject matter then evaluate the instructional materials. A standardized rating form is desirable for the assessment (for an example, see Exhibit 4).

Another successful approach is to have a colleague who teaches the same subject join forces with a colleague who teaches outside the discipline to examine the course outline and teaching materials. The two render judgments on the accuracy, soundness, academic level, and relationship to course objectives of the materials. The judgments are shared with the instructor, who can comment in writing on them. Both the judgments and the comments are transmitted to the academic dean and department head.

Classroom Visitation to Improve Performance. Colleague observation of classroom instruction can be an effective way to improve teaching. The visitation poses minimal threat, since the instructor being observed has a say in the selection of the visitation date, behaviors to be observed, and conditions of observation. If the initiative for the visitation comes from the instructor, so much the better. A classroom observation procedure, as part of the overall teaching improvement program, is offered by Berquist and Phillips (1975). It consists of a peer observer from the same department or, if the instructor prefers, from a different department. The observer attends several class sessions during the semester. After each session, the teaching is rated for the employment of specific teaching strategies and the instructor's performance. There are also a general evaluation and open-end comments. After each session, the observer meets with the instructor to identify teaching strengths and weaknesses and to discuss ways to strengthen performance. Which teaching characteristics should an observer watch for? An observer's guide containing more than 200 items was developed by Helling (1976). The following sample items deal with lecture and discussion formats:

Teaching by Lecture

- Uses illustrative material or teaching aids.
- Is sensitive to response of class.
- Refers to recent developments in the field.
- Focuses student attention before starting lecture.
- Refers back to points made or terms used earlier.
- Summarizes major points or sees that class does so.
- Appears interested and enthusiastic.
- Uses humor.
- Accepts student ideas and comments.
- Provides opportunities and encourages student questions.
- Includes material relevant to existing student interest.

Teaching by Discussion

- Lets students know what is to be expected of them.
- Draws together contributions of group members.
- Uses questions to stimulate discussion.
- Prevents or terminates discussion monopolies.
- Reinforces infrequent contributors.
- Reminds students to listen to each other.
- If discussion falters, stops to deal with group process.
- Intervenes briefly when necessary.
- Questions misconceptions, faulty logic, unwarranted conclusions.
- Distinguishes a value from a fact.
- Intervenes when discussion gets off track.
- Supports expression of differences of opinion.

Improved teaching performance is more likely after classroom visitation if (1) a climate of candor and trust exists among the faculty; (2) the observer is trained in observation techniques; (3) the observer's findings are discussed in an informal, objective, descriptive manner; (4) the instructor does not get defensive. Experience suggests the advantage of younger and older faculty members working together as a team to assess performance. Another successful approach depends on the designation of an instructor as a master teacher. Such an instructor, given a reduced teaching load, serves as classroom observer for all colleagues.

Classroom Visitation for Personnel Decisions. Generally, colleges and universities enjoy more success with classroom visitation when its purpose is to improve teaching, not to influence personnel decisions. Major problems inhere in classroom observation for personnel decisions. For example:

1. Classroom observation is perceived by many faculty as both an invasion of privacy and a violation of academic freedom.
2. The instructor's performance may be weakened by anxiety or strengthened by special preparation.
3. Classroom visitation makes severe demands on faculty time and energy.
4. It is often afflicted by problems of sampling and rater unreliability.
5. Peer ratings tend to be high, due perhaps to an unspoken wish for reciprocity.
6. At most colleges and universities, the level of mutual trust, respect, and rapport among faculty members necessary for meaningful classroom observation by colleagues is unavailable.

Despite these depressing negatives, some institutions are successful in using classroom observation for tenure and promotion decisions. How is it done? They employ classroom observation as a part of the entire performance evaluation. They rely on several colleagues to make classroom visits several times to dilute possible individual bias or atypical teaching performance. The observers are extensively trained. In short, successful use of classroom observation for tenure and promotion decisions is characterized by planning, training, open communication, feedback, and trust.

Conducting the Observation. If the observer brings blank

paper and pencil to the classroom, the likelihood is that the ensuing random notes will prove of little or no value to a personnel committee making a tenure or promotion decision. What is required is a standardized evaluation instrument. What questions will help zero in on quality of performance?

Structure and Goals. Does the instructor's presentation show clear signs of planning and organization? Are the various instructional elements (lecture, blackboard material, handouts) effectively integrated? Is the class time used efficiently? Is the material presented effectively? Does the instructor respond appropriately to unanticipated situations?

Teaching Behaviors. Does the instructor maintain sufficient eye contact with students? Is the oral delivery too rapid, too slow? Does the instructor exhibit distracting mannerisms? Is the language used understandable to students? Is the instructor active enough? Too active?

Instructor–Student Rapport. Does the instructor demonstrate fair and equitable concern for all students? Do the students seem receptive to the instructor's ideas? Are student questions answered clearly and simply? Is the instructor sarcastic to students? How would you describe the instructor–student relationship?

Subject Matter and Instruction. Does the instructor demonstrate adequate knowledge of the subject? Is the instructor up to date in the discipline? Are the transitions between topics effective? Is the course material presented in a lively and interesting style? Is the material appropriate for course and student level? Are the students generally attentive? Does the instructor demonstrate enthusiasm for the subject? For teaching?

General. Do you believe you can properly judge the teaching-learning process in the classroom visited? Would you recommend this instructor to students advised by you? Why or why not? What specific changes are needed to strengthen teaching performance? How would you rate this instructor against others teaching similar courses in the department?

The standardized observation instrument should include questions specific enough to generate comparative information. A point-range system is a simple response format, but there should also be sufficient space for open-end questions. Integrity demands that the intended use of the observer's findings be candidly discussed by observer and instructor. The classroom visitation program will rise or fall on the unreserved acceptance of the intrinsic fairness of the evaluation instrument and process. Even a few serious misgivings place the program at risk.

Which faculty members should be selected as observers? Preferably, they will be tenured senior colleagues chosen by the department chair (or by the academic dean in consultation with the department chair). At some institutions, the teacher is requested to submit the names of five or six colleagues, and the department chair selects three of the names. Those chosen should each possess a campus reputation as a gifted and respected teacher and be noted for sensitivity, tact, and the ability to get along with people. If they lack the skills, they should be trained as observers.

Several days prior to the visitation, the observers should meet with the instructor to review the content and teaching methods planned for the class to be observed. The observers should be in the class before it begins and remain for the full period. A standardized appraisal form should be used (for example, see Exhibits 5 and 6) and reviewed with the instructor before the observation. Two or three days after the visitation, the observers should discuss with the instructor their tentative conclusions and recommendations. The instructor should be invited to comment on the conclusions and recommendations. If the observation was intended for personnel decision, the written report should include the instructor's comments before submission to the department chair.

Self-Evaluation

Almost all faculty members assess their own teaching performance partly from student reactions and partly from student achievement on examinations. Some faculty members go a step further and complete self-evaluation forms.

Self-Evaluation to Improve Performance. Generally, institutions find self-evaluation more useful as a tool to improve teaching than as an aid in personnel decisions. Instructors recognize that, no matter what they disclose in self-evaluations, it will serve to improve their performance and not be held against them. Self-evaluations, therefore, can theoretically be completely honest. However, self-evaluation is not always a straight road to improvement. Some instructors simply do not know how to evaluate their own performance meaningfully. Some know their strong and weak areas but do not know what to do with the information. Some live with the illusion that they are quintessential teachers. What techniques are available to teachers for self-evaluation?

Audio and Video Recording. Watching and listening to their own taped classroom performances help teachers to identify the pluses and minuses in their performance and to view themselves a bit more objectively. Most teachers, however, need faculty colleagues or teaching-improvement specialists to assist in the analysis and to suggest appropriate changes. It is also helpful for teachers to be able to compare their performance with models of good teaching. Although both audio and visual replays are useful, the video portion is probably more useful, since the reactions of students can also be observed. One caution, however: Because they are inherently self-confrontational, audio and visual replays also have the potential for harm. Teachers who submit to videotaping over their objections or have teaching limitations beyond remedy may be adversely affected.

Student Rating and Self-Rating. In some colleges and universities, after the students have completed the evaluation form, the teachers complete the same form. The teachers subsequently complete the form again, but this time by predicting how they were rated by the students. Comparing these two evaluations by the teachers and examining the actual student evaluation can be revelatory. Any sharp discrepancy among the three ratings signals the need for a second, closer look.

Faculty Growth Contracts. Self-evaluation plays a key role in a faculty growth contract. The contract is prepared by the instructor in writing and spells out in specific terms (1) the instructor's academic goals for the year, (2) the plan to achieve each goal, and (3) the budget required to achieve the goals. In brief, the contract charts the direction of professional growth and the specifics for measuring achievements at year-end. Since they are individually tailored, the growth contracts tend to turn teachers inward to reflect on their strong and weak points as teachers. At year-end, they will know how they measured up to their stipulated growth expectation and goal achievements, and the stage can be set for the next year.

The growth contracts rest on the double assumption that instructors know their shortcomings and are also intent on overcoming them. To write the contracts, the instructors first have to identify their strengths and weaknesses. Then they list in detail their institutional and community responsibilities and their long-range personal and professional goals and assess their current responsibilities and the improvements to be worked for during the period of the contract. In the writing of the contracts and their monitoring at year-end, the instructors work closely with the academic dean or department chair. As each instructor grows, so does the entire staff.

Self-Evaluation for Personnel Decisions. Some institutions employ self-evaluation for personnel decisions, since it adds another piece of evidence to consider in the committee's collective judgment. There is value in a candid self-appraisal and explanation of teaching virtues and faults. To be truly useful in personnel decisions, however, self-evaluation requires a standardized format and a spelling out in hard-nosed language of the accomplishments and failures during the year. Solid evidence of accomplishments must be presented. Solid explanations for shortcomings and/or failures must also be readily available. Even then, self-evaluation as an instrument for change can be mercurial, and institutions should consider it only as a component of an evaluative system. It cannot be trusted alone to be the basis for personnel decisions.

Regrettably, many colleges and universities are today making use of faculty activity sheets for tenure, promotion, and retention decisions. The problem is that the data on these activity sheets are vague and self-serving. They show what professors did rather than how well they think they did it. They are self-reports rather than self-assessments. They lack credentials for personnel decisions.

Guiding Questions. Guiding questions are needed both to encourage modest teachers to state their accomplishments and to discourage pretentious teachers from inflating them.

Discipline and Classroom Approach. Within your discipline, which area do you regard as your strongest? Your weakest? What is your greatest asset as a classroom teacher? Your greatest shortcoming? Which teaching approach works best for your discipline? Why? Do you change methods to meet new classroom situations? Can you give a recent example? What is your primary goal with respect to your students?

Instructor–Student Rapport. How would you describe the feeling between you and your students? How would you describe the atmosphere in your classroom? Are you satisfied with it? Do you tolerate honest disagreements? In your teaching, do you have any covert or do you express any overt hostility to students? When? Do your students consider you sarcastic?

Knowledge of Discipline. In what ways have you tried to stay current in your field? How would you judge your knowledge in the subjects you teach? Do you think your colleagues agree with that judgment? What could you do to broaden and deepen your knowledge of the discipline?

Questions About Teaching. What would you like most to hear from your students? From your colleagues? What do you like most about teaching? Least? What kind of activities take place in your classroom? Why? What is the one thing that you most want your students to learn? Why? What is the one thing that you would most like to change about your teaching? What have you done about changing it? What would you most like your students to remember about you as a teacher ten years from now? Overall, how effective do you think you are as a teacher? Would your colleagues agree? Your students? Which courses do you teach most effectively? In what ways has your teaching changed in the last five years? Ten years? Are these changes for the better? Why or why not?

A checklist of questions for instructors preparing for a new semester was developed by Cleary (n.d.). The following items are excerpted from that checklist.

- Would it help to weave more contemporary or real-world material into the course?
- Have I relied for too many years on the same dog-eared notes or tired, dated textbook?

- How heavy a work load can I reasonably impose?
- What is the value of the course and my ways of teaching it?
- Do students truly learn by preparing for my tests or merely prepare themselves to survive them?
- Should I encourage group or collaborative effort on assignments?
- Are my comments on the content, organization, and style of papers and examinations legible, clear, and helpful?
- What is my policy for dealing with plagiarism and cheating? Is it consistent with that of the department?
- How promptly do I grade and return assignments?
- Where do I draw the line between acceptable absenteeism and abuse?
- Am I easy to talk to, easy to make a mistake in front of?
- How available will I be — should I be — outside of class?
- What have I learned about myself or the course that needs to be changed this year?

For the purpose of personnel decision, self-evaluation forms should contain both general and summary items and be judgmental in character. For the purpose of teaching improvement, self-evaluation forms should zero in on specific and diagnostic questions (for examples, see Exhibits 7, 8, and 9).

Together with student ratings, colleague assessment, and self-evaluation, the comprehensive faculty evaluation system should also include additional sources of information. Some of these are informal student opinion, student performance on examinations, department chair and academic dean evaluations, alumni opinions, enrollment in elective courses, long-term follow-up of students, and faculty participation in teaching-improvement activities. Each source can contribute to an understanding of what goes on behind a closed classroom door. But each source needs weighing in terms of the institution's needs, local politics, and available cost and time. No college or university would want to use every source. Each institution must weigh these elements on its own scales. No two scales are exactly alike.

Evaluating Institutional and Community Service

It is a widely accepted notion in colleges and universities that among faculty responsibilities is service to the institution and to the nonacademic community.

Institutional Service

Service to the institution, like other academic activities, should be evaluated in terms of what it is and how well it is accomplished. *Institutional service* is an umbrella phrase covering a wide range of activities, such as

1.   serving on departmental and institutional committees,
2.   screening candidates for faculty and administrative positions,
3.   participating in student recruitment,
4.   serving on the academic senate and its committees,
5.   counseling students during the academic year,
6.   assisting in student orientation and registration,
7.   serving as faculty adviser to student organizations,
8.   serving as the designated representative of the institution.

Some institutions specify service at every level—department, college, university—as a minimal contribution. Others specify a percentage of faculty time to be spent in service to the institution. Still others designate student advising as the only required institutional service. A willingness to carry an extra work load or to include a less desirable course in the teaching load may be considered service. For judgments on the quality of service, standard rating forms should be used (for example, see Exhibit 10). The following lines of inquiry may be helpful:

Committee Work. Does the instructor attend regularly? Contribute actively to the work of the group? Are committee assignments accepted willingly? Is the committee better because of this instructor's participation? Do other committee members share this appraisal?

Committee Chair. Is this person an effective chair? Are meetings called only for a specific purpose? Does the chair make appropriate use of each committee member's special expertise? Are passive members encouraged and aggressive members restrained? How skillfully? Has the chair arranged for committee minutes to be taken? Is needed material distributed to members to be read and considered in advance of the meeting?

Attitude Toward Institutional Service. Does the instructor willingly execute assignments? Volunteer to take on service tasks? How responsive is the instructor to the needs of the department? The institution?

General. How do you rate this instructor's service against others in the department? In the institution? What is needed to improve the quality of that contribution (workshops or training seminars)?

Ordinarily, the department chair and faculty colleagues are in advantageous positions to judge the quality of institutional service. In smaller institutions, the academic dean may also be in such a position. The judgments should be based on personal observation over a long time.

Community Service

Community service is profession-related work performed by faculty in settings outside the institution. It may be working for government agencies, delivering speeches to community groups, or applying teaching and research expertise to community concerns. At times, a community service project can endure beyond the academic year and involve responsibility for developing and coordinating a major community endeavor. Other projects may end in a few months or a few days. Information about community service comes mainly from the instructor's own vita. The information should be supported whenever possible by documentation.

Although community service is considered a valuable and proper role for a faculty member, it is not included by most institutions in tenure and promotion decisions. At some institutions, community service is regarded as lightweight. However, in an age of suddenly stepped-up institutional and faculty accountability, community service may find itself in time upgraded to heavyweight.

Evaluating Research and Publication

Most colleges and universities give a full measure of importance to research and publication in rendering tenure and promotion decisions, but the practice varies. Some institutions relieve instructors of many customary responsibilities when they are engaged in major research. Some do not expect teachers dedicated to the classroom to find time for research and publication. But most institutions expect their instructors to be both dedicated to the classroom and solidly involved in research and publication. They are accountable in both areas.

Institutions relying on a publish-or-perish philosophy for tenure and promotion decisions too often simply count the instructor's published articles. This procedure ignores quality. Its faulty assumption is that one article is as good as another. Any instructor eager to publish in quantity has a growing number of journals as a marketplace. Ulrich's *International Periodical Directory* listed 28,000 titles in 1965, 57,000 in 1975, and 63,000 in 1981. The 1981 edition of the *Directory of Publishing Opportunities* lists more than 3,900 specialized and professional journals accepting manuscripts in English. For personnel review committees, the multiplicity of journals raises the often unanswerable question: What does publication in a particular journal mean? Committee members sometimes have never heard of the journal. They have no way of judging its worth or the worth of the article cited in the instructor's vitae.

What criteria should be used in evaluating journals? Who should do the evaluating? Winkler (1982) suggests as an index of a journal's importance its frequency of use. A committee of the American Library Association proposes the ranking of journals by the number of subscribers. The Institute for Scientific Information (Philadelphia) adds up the citations of an article in a particular journal by other writers. The last approach invites problems of its own. The citations may be numerous but predominantly negative. The significance of the article may take years to gain full recognition. The time lag between an article's acceptance and its printing may be years, to which must be added the time lag in the updating of the citation index.

It has been argued that any article in a refereed journal is per se a quality article. The problem is that refereed journals are subject to editorial needs of the moment, varying standards, and a degree of human fallibility. And there are many excellent non-refereed journals. Even the quality of research papers may not be easy to assess. Cole, Cole, and Simon (1981, p. 883), in an analysis of scientific research, conclude: "Contrary to a widely held belief that science is characterized by wide agreement about what is good work. . . there is substantial disagreement in all scientific fields." The comment appears in *Science*, a refereed journal. The problem remains thorny.

Although the ultimate practices vary, colleges and universities face the same set of core problems when they set out to develop a system to evaluate research and publication. They include the following questions:

1. When several faculty members coauthor an article, how is the contribution of each to be weighed?
2. How are the articles to be valued if based on theoretical considerations rather than research studies?
3. Does the institution prefer basic or applied research, and how is each to be weighed?
4. How is the institution to assess research spanning several years if a tenure/promotion decision must be made before the research is completed?
5. Must the research be directly related to the professor's teaching area?

Some institutions solicit judgments of a professor's peers in the same field but at other institutions. Depending on how it is done, the solicitation can produce assessments even more objective than from colleagues in the same institution, who may be unduly influenced by friendship or rivalry. In seeking opinions from colleagues outside the institution, it is generally more productive to specify topic areas than to ask for an overall estimation of a professor. Such topics might include the quality and importance of the professor's publications, national reputation and relative standing in the discipline, and whether the professor is ascending, leveling off, or falling in professional reputation. However, rather than seek the judgments of outsiders, most institutions rely on the professor's colleagues in the department; sometimes the department chair is solicited, and the professor is asked for a self-assessment.

Publication patterns appear to vary by academic discipline and in time. Centra (1979) reports that faculty members in the natural sciences publish more frequently early in their academic careers than do those in the humanities or social sciences but that the situation reverses itself twelve years later. This finding may be of special importance to the many institutions opening a certain number of promotion/tenure slots to institutionwide competition. Natural science professors might have the edge within the first six years, when most tenure decisions are made. On the other hand, the slight competitive advantage swings to professors in the humanities and social sciences in later years, when they apply for promotion to senior rank.

The fact is that there is a dearth of research-based instruments available to assess a professor's research and publication performance. And they are generally similar in approach. They ask questions requiring specific answers, include a point-range scale of 1–5 or 1–7, and ask questions requiring open-end answers (for examples, see Exhibits 11 and 12). What kind of information is used to evaluate a professor's research/scholarship performance? The list might include the following:

1.   publication in professional journals,
2.   articles in high-quality journals,
3.   papers at professional meetings,
4.   citations in published material of others,
5.   books as sole or senior author,
6.   books as junior author or editor,
7.   monographs or chapters in books,
8.   unpublished research leading to new knowledge or new applications of existing knowledge,
9.   editing professional journals,
10. serving as referee on professional journals or as reviewer of papers presented at professional meetings,

11.   reviewing textbooks for publishers,
12.   participating in meetings or conferences of professional associations,
13.   writing grant proposals for research projects.

The above list contains items incompatible with the objectives of some institutions. It is left to each institution to tailor the list to its own local needs. It is not intended as a Procrustean bed into which all institutions must fit. If there is one common denominator, however, it is that faculty confidence in whatever rating system is developed is the key to the system's faculty support.

A Final Word About Faculty Evaluation

It is always easier to raise questions about faculty evaluation than to offer answers. Nonetheless, equipped with hindsight and the benefit of research, we know many more things today than we knew a decade ago, even a year or two ago. We know that:

1.   Faculty evaluation is a complex process, and no single source of data is adequate. The combined appraisals of students, colleagues, administrators, and the professor's self-assessment are required for reasonably reliable and valid judgments.
2.   Faculty evaluation is an evolving process, and any component infrequently used today may be frequently used tomorrow.
3.   Fairness requires the criteria, standards, and evidence used by an institution to be disseminated clearly, fully, and in writing to every faculty member.
4.   Faculty evaluation is both a process and a result: a way to determine goals, to appraise the processes for reaching them, and to assess the extent to which they have been met.
5.   The faculty evaluation program must be administratively manageable and cost and time efficient.
6.   The program must provide active administrative support to improve faculty performance.
7.   Many professors genuinely fear that disclosures from evaluation for improvement will be misapplied to tenure, promotion, and retention decisions.

8.   The cornerstone of the program is its acceptance by the faculty, which rests on faculty confidence in the program's integrity, which in turn rests in part on the faculty's active participation in the program's development.

9.   Many professors find it awkward and disturbing to appraise colleague performance and require training for the task.

10. The program must be designed to include reviews so that inappropriate or biased items can be eliminated during the evaluative process.

11. Evaluation programs used for tenure, promotion, and retention decisions must include an appeals procedure to assure a fairer result.

12. Due process must be built into the program to safeguard the legal rights of professors in tenure, promotion, and retention decisions.

13. There is no perfect evaluation program, nor can there be. Such a system will probably always remain beyond reach. But with enough time, effort, and goodwill, we can come reasonably close.

The following general guidelines have been developed from experience as an aid to institutions in evolving faculty evaluation procedures. The guidelines will help point the way to successful evaluation programs.

1.   Obtain the active support and involvement of top-level administrators.

2.   Obtain widespread faculty involvement in every step of the program's development. It is essential for faculty members to believe they control their own destiny.

3.   Decide on the specific roles played by administrators, faculty members, the faculty senate, students, and, if applicable, representatives of the faculty union and the board of trustees. (Usually, representatives of each segment of the academic community are appointed to a central coordinating committee.)

4.   Pay scrupulous attention to campus protocol. Knowing how to thread its way through the administrative/faculty gover-

nance maze is especially important for the faculty evaluation coordinating committee.

5. Hold open forums during the developmental stage of the rating instruments, methods, and procedures. Encourage the student newspaper to report on the meetings.
6. Determine objectives and uses of the evaluation data.
7. Determine the who, what, where, and when in the implementation of the evaluation system as well as the specific roles of administrators, faculty members, and students.
8. Keep all segments of the campus community informed on a continuing basis. Two-way communication is vital to the coordinating committee. For example, many committees report periodically on their activities and progress at general faculty meetings and in newsletters.
9. Anticipate faculty resistance and deal with it sympathetically by demonstrating understanding. Use a trade-off approach to emphasize the benefits to faculty in improved performance.
10. Determine the financing of the faculty evaluation system.
11. Establish an office to administer the faculty evaluation program. If the assessment data are to be used for personnel decisions, the faculty development office should not serve as the administrative body.
12. Allow sufficient time to implement the system, and work diligently to develop a solid research base and to demonstrate genuine enthusiasm for the program.
13. Conduct dry runs to improve the rating instruments and administrative procedures.
14. Carry out follow-up studies to assess the effectiveness of the program and to improve it.
15. Tie faculty evaluation to overall efforts for the recognition, reward, and improvement of faculty performance.

The key to developing successful faculty evaluation programs is to proceed slowly, carefully, openly, and to lay the groundwork for each step in the program. Success does not come easily, but it comes. The proof is in the successful evaluation programs operating around the country.

Exhibit 1. Student Report on Teaching.

Instructor: _____ Course: _____ Date: _____

Please report your impressions of the professor in this course by using the rating scale listed below. Please be as objective and honest in your responses as possible.

Strongly Agree = SA
Agree = A
Disagree = D
Strongly Disagree = SD
Not Applicable = NA

The Professor:

1.	was well prepared for class.	SA	A	D	SD	NA
2.	clearly indicated material the graded work would cover.	SA	A	D	SD	NA
3.	gave students adequate information on their progress.	SA	A	D	SD	NA
4.	organized class well on a daily basis.	SA	A	D	SD	NA
5.	stimulated interest in the subject.	SA	A	D	SD	NA
6.	effectively encouraged class discussion.	SA	A	D	SD	NA
7.	clearly presented abstract ideas and theories.	SA	A	D	SD	NA
8.	invited criticism or comment on the ideas presented.	SA	A	D	SD	NA
9.	was concerned that students learn and understand.	SA	A	D	SD	NA
10.	was available for individual help.	SA	A	D	SD	NA
11.	demonstrated enthusiasm for teaching.	SA	A	D	SD	NA
12.	was one of the best I have had at this college.	SA	A	D	SD	NA

PLEASE COMMENT FURTHER ON THESE POINTS OR OTHERS IN THE SPACE BELOW.

Exhibit 2. Student Questionnaire: Report on Teaching.

Instructor: _____ Course: _____ Date: _____

Please take a few minutes to seriously consider and complete this form. It will be used to compile a Student Report on Teaching, which will be used as a part of the regular process of faculty evaluation. Space is provided on this report form for optional items selected by the department or the faculty member.

Your response to each item below should be a number from 5 to 1, or you may leave the item blank if you are unable to respond or feel that the item does not apply. Rate each item according to the following scale.

STRONGLY AGREE   5   4   3   2   1   STRONGLY DISAGREE

Place your rating in the space to the left of each statement.

Course

_____ 1. The objectives of this course were made clear.

_____ 2. My course responsibilities were clearly defined.

_____ 3. The teaching materials required for this course were helpful.

_____ 4. The methods of evaluation (examinations, papers, projects, class discussions) were relevant and representative of the total course content.

_____ 5. I have been graded fairly and accurately.

_____ 6. Overall, the course was of value to me.

Instructor

_____ 7. The instructor's classroom sessions were stimulating.

_____ 8. The instructor communicated the subject matter effectively.

_____ 9. The instructor showed enthusiasm for the subject.

_____ 10. The instructor was well prepared for class.

_____ 11. The instructor encouraged and was responsive to student participation.

_____ 12. The instructor made adequate provision for consultation and assistance.

_____ 13. The instructor showed an interest in and respect for me as an individual.

_____ 14. I would recommend this instructor to other students.

_____ 15. I would rate the instructor as an excellent teacher.

_____ 16.

_____ 17.

_____ 18.

_____ 19.

_____ 20.

continued on following page

Exhibit 2. Student Questionnaire: Report on Teaching *(continued).*

COMMENT ITEMS

21.   Describe strengths of this class and/or instructor; try to be specific;
      use examples.

22.   Describe weaknesses of this class and/or instructor; try to be specific;
      use examples.

23.   What changes would you recommend for this class and/or instructor?
      Any other comments?

Exhibit 3. Student Report on Instruction.

Faculty member: _____ Term: _____

Course: _____ Department: _____

Please indicate your appraisal of the instructor's performance in this class by drawing a circle around the number that most closely expresses your view. Do not sign your name. Your thoughtful attention to the items on this form is sincerely appreciated.

		Strongly Agree				*Strongly Disagree*	*Don't Know*
1.	The objectives of this course were clearly explained.	1	2	3	4	5	X
2.	In-class activities were relevant to the objectives of the course.	1	2	3	4	5	X
3.	The instructor was well prepared for class sessions.	1	2	3	4	5	X
4.	The grading system was a fair way to measure knowledge/ ability.	1	2	3	4	5	X
5.	This course aroused my curiosity and challenged me intellectually.	1	2	3	4	5	X
6.	The instructor was helpful when students had difficulty with course material.	1	2	3	4	5	X
7.	The instructor was available and willing to consult with students during office hours.	1	2	3	4	5	X

OVERALL EVALUATION

8.	The instructor was one of the best I have had at this college.	1	2	3	4	5	X
9.	The course was one of the best I have had at this college.	1	2	3	4	5	X

YOUR FURTHER COMMENTS ARE INVITED:

_____

_____

_____

_____

_____

Exhibit 4. Peer Evaluation of Teaching Materials.

Listed below are items concerned with teaching materials. They are categorized into three major areas. For each item, indicate on a five-point scale (1–5, with 5 being high) the extent to which the materials meet the criteria as represented by each item.

Course Organization.

____ The syllabus adequately outlines the sequence of topics to be covered.
____ The stated course objectives are clear.
____ The outline and sequence of topics are logical.
____ The difficulty level is appropriate for the enrolled students.
____ The course integrates recent developments in the field.
____ Time given to each of the major course topics is appropriate.
____ The course is responsive to the needs of the enrolled students.
____ The course is an adequate prerequisite for other courses.
____ The course objectives are congruent with the department curricula.

Readings, Projects, and Laboratory Assignments.

____ The reading list (required/recommended) is up to date and represents the work of recognized authorities.
____ Readings are appropriate for level of course.
____ The texts used in the course are well selected.
____ Students are given ample time to complete the assignments/take-home exams.
____ The amount of homework and assignments is appropriate.
____ The written assignments and projects are carefully chosen to reflect course goals.
____ A variety of assignments is available to meet individual student needs.
____ Laboratory work is integrated into the course.
____ Students are given the course requirements in writing at the beginning of the course.
____ The assignments are intellectually challenging to the students.

Exams and Grading.

____ The exam content is representative of the course content and objectives.
____ The exam items are clear and well written.
____ The exams are graded in a fair manner.
____ The grade distribution is appropriate for the level of course and type of students enrolled.
____ The standards used for grading are communicated to the students.

Source: Braskamp and others, 1983. Reproduced by permission.

Exhibit 5. Classroom Observation Report.

Instructor evaluated _____ Course _____

Number of students present _____ Date _____

Evaluator(s) _____

Purpose: The purpose of this classroom observation is (1) to provide a data base for more accurate and equitable decisions on tenure, promotion, and merit increase and (2) to improve faculty performance.

Instructions: Please consider each item carefully and assign the highest scores only for unusually effective performance.

Questions 12 and 13 have been deliberately left blank. You and the instructor being evaluated are encouraged to add your own items.

Each instructor should be observed on two occasions, and the observer(s) should remain in the classroom for the full class period.

It is suggested that the observer(s) arrange a previsit and postvisit meeting with the instructor.

Highest		*Satisfactory*		*Lowest*	*Not Applicable*
5	4	3	2	1	n/a

_____ 1. Defines objectives for the class presentation.

_____ 2. Effectively organizes learning situations to meet the objectives of the class presentation.

_____ 3. Uses instructional methods encouraging relevant student participation in the learning process.

_____ 4. Uses class time effectively.

_____ 5. Demonstrates enthusiasm for the subject matter.

_____ 6. Communicates clearly and effectively to the level of the students.

_____ 7. Explains important ideas simply and clearly.

_____ 8. Demonstrates command of subject matter.

_____ 9. Responds appropriately to student questions and comments.

_____ 10. Encourages critical thinking and analysis.

_____ 11. Considering the previous items, how would you rate this instructor in comparison to others in the department?

_____ 12.

_____ 13.

_____ 14. Overall rating

continued on following page

Exhibit 5. Classroom Observation Report *(continued).*

Would you recommend this instructor to students you are advising? (Please explain.)

What specific suggestions would you make concerning how this particular class could have been improved?

Did you have a previsit conference? _____ postvisit conference? _____

Source: Seldin, 1980. Reproduced by permission.

Exhibit 6. Report of Classroom Observation.

Instructor: _____ Course: _____

Number of students present: _____ Date: _____

Observer(s):_____

INSTRUCTIONS: Several days prior to the classroom observation, the instructor should provide the observer(s) with a copy of the course syllabus containing course objectives, content, and organization. The instructor should explain to the observer(s) the instructional goals and methods of accomplishing them for the class that will be observed.

Within three days after the visit, the observer(s) should meet with the instructor to discuss observations and conclusions.

Please use the reverse side of this page to elaborate on your comments.

1. Describe the lesson taught, including the subject, objectives, and methods used.

2. Describe the instructor's teaching as it relates to content mastery, breadth, and depth.

3. How well organized and clear is the presentation?

4. How appropriate were the teaching techniques used for the instructor's goals for this class?

5. Describe the level of student interest and participation.

6. What are the instructor's major strengths? Weaknesses?

7. What specific recommendations would you make to improve the instructor's teaching in this class?

Exhibit 7. Faculty Self-Evaluation of Overall Performance.

Name_____ Department _____ Date_____

If more space is needed, please use reverse side of page.

1. In which area of your discipline do you consider yourself strongest?

2. What is your greatest strength as a teacher? Your greatest weakness?

3. If you could change one thing, what would you most like to change about your teaching?

4. Compared to others in your department, how do you assess your teaching performance?

5. What was your most important accomplishment as a faculty member in the past year?

6. Compared to others in your department, how do you assess that accomplishment?

7. Compared to others in your department, how do you assess your research and publication activity? You contribution to the institution? To the community?

8. Considering your answers to the previous questions, how do you assess your overall performance as a faculty member in your department?

Exhibit 8. Instructor Self-Evaluation Report on Teaching.

Professor:_____ Department:_____

DIRECTIONS

Following are a number of statements describing some aspects of college teaching. These statements are listed in sets of four. We would like you to examine the items in each set and rank them from 1 to 4 as to the degree to which they apply to you and your course.

In responding, first examine the set and find the item that describes you or your course *most* and assign a rank of 1 to that statement. Then decide which statement describes you or your own course second-best, and assign a rank of 2 to that item. Do likewise with the two remaining statements, assigning to them ranks of 3 and 4 depending on their degree of applicability to you or your own course.

If you find some items difficult to rank, please show what your choices would be if you have to choose. It is important that you assign a different rank to each item.

Here is an example:

____1____	a.	I present ideas clearly in class.
____3____	b.	I enjoy teaching my own course.
____2____	c.	I stimulate students' interest in the subject.
____4____	d.	I am fair and impartial in dealing with students.

The person responding to that set indicated that item a. was most descriptive of him (rank of 1), while item c. was thought to be second most descriptive (rank of 2). Items b. and d. were given ranks of 3 and 4, respectively, as they applied at least to that instructor. You may wish to respond to the questionnaire having in mind one particular course or the totality of the courses that you teach.

Note: The form that follows, unlike the others in this book, is experimental in nature and was designed solely for use in improving instruction rather than evaluating it for purposes of personnel decision.

Set 1

_____	a.	I present thought-provoking ideas.
_____	b.	I am sympathetic toward and considerate of students.
_____	c.	I assist students in appreciating things they did not appreciate before.
_____	d.	I am interested in and concerned with the quality of my teaching.

continued on following page

Exhibit 8. Instructor Self-Evaluation Report on Teaching *(continued).*

Set 2

_____ a. My students feel efforts made by them in the course are worthwhile.

_____ b. I am aware of students' needs.

_____ c. I raise challenging questions or problems in class.

_____ d. I make every effort to improve the quality of students' achievement in my course.

Set 3

_____ a. I encourage students to share in class their knowledge, opinions, and experiences.

_____ b. I help students become aware of the implications of the course's subject matter in their life.

_____ c. I remind students to come to me for help whenever it is needed.

_____ d. I analyze previous classroom experience to improve my teaching.

Set 4

_____ a. I take an active, personal interest in improving my instruction.

_____ b. I stimulate and answer questions in class.

_____ c. I relate to students easily.

_____ d. I help students to develop the ability to marshal or identify main points or central issues.

Set 5

_____ a. I organize my course well.

_____ b. I am knowledgeable about related areas aside from my own.

_____ c. I stimulate students' appreciation for the subject.

_____ d. I get along well with students.

Set 6

_____ a. I restate questions or comments to clarify them for the entire class.

_____ b. I try to make every course the best every time.

_____ c. I am sensitive to students' feelings.

_____ d. I promote students' satisfaction in learning the subject matter.

Set 7

_____ a. My students gain new viewpoints and appreciations.

_____ b. I have zest and enthusiasm for teaching.

continued on following page

Exhibit 8. Instructor Self-Evaluation Report on Teaching *(continued)*.

_____ c.   I develop a sense of mutual respect with students.

_____ d.   I present clear and relevant examples in class.

Set 8

_____ a.   I find teaching intellectually stimulating.

_____ b.   I make students feel at ease in conversations with me.

_____ c.   I stimulate students' interest in the subject.

_____ d.   I answer questions as thoroughly and precisely as possible.

Set 9

_____ a.   I coordinate different activities of my course well.

_____ b.   I look forward to class meetings.

_____ c.   I enjoy having students come to me for consultation.

_____ d.   My students feel that they can recognize good and poor reasoning or arguments in the field.

Set 10

_____ a.   I try to function creatively in teaching my course.

_____ b.   I encourage students to participate in class.

_____ c.   I actively help students who are having difficulties.

_____ d.   I stimulate students' intellectual curiosity.

Set 11

_____ a.   I meet with students informally out of class when necessary.

_____ b.   I make the objectives of the course clear.

_____ c.   I try to make every course the best every time.

_____ d.   My students become motivated to study and learn.

Scoring the Instructor Self-Evaluation Form (ISEF)

The ISEF has four subscales:

1.   Adequacy of Classroom Procedures.
2.   Enthusiasm for Teaching and Knowledge of Subject Matter.

continued on following page

Exhibit 8. Instructor Self-Evaluation Report on Teaching *(continued).*

3.   Stimulation of Cognitive and Affective Gains in Students.
4.   Relations with Students.

One statement from each of the eleven tetrads is associated with each subscale. Scoring is determined by first reversing the ranks given to each statement within a tetrad (for example, rank of $1 = 4$) and then adding the reversed numbers across the eleven tetrads. The statements belonging to each subscale by tetrad are as follows:

Set 1		*Set 4*		*Set 7*		*Set 10*	
a.	1	a.	2	a.	3	a.	2
b.	4	b.	1	b.	2	b.	1
c.	3	c.	4	c.	4	c.	4
d.	2	d.	3	d.	1	d.	3
Set 2		*Set 5*		*Set 8*		*Set 11*	
a.	3	a.	1	a.	2	a.	4
b.	4	b.	2	b.	4	b.	1
c.	1	c.	3	c.	3	c.	2
d.	2	d.	4	d.	1	d.	3
Set 3		*Set 6*		*Set 9*			
a.	1	a.	1	a.	1		
b.	3	b.	2	b.	2		
c.	4	c.	4	c.	4		
d.	2	d.	3	d.	3		

For illustration, suppose that the ranks assigned for set 1 were as follows:

Statement	*Rank*	*Score*
a.	4	1
b.	2	3
c.	1	4
d.	3	2

Statement a. belongs to subscale 1 and was given a rank of 4. Reversing the rank yields a score of 1 to be added to the subscale 1 total. Statement b. belongs to subscale 4 and was given a rank of 2, and so on. Adding across all eleven tetrads yields a maximum score of 44 for a given subscale or a minimum of 11. A score of 44 would mean that each statement in the tetrad was assigned the highest priority by that individual.

Source: Braskamp and others, 1983. Further information about the ISEF may be obtained by contacting Dale C. Brandenburg, Coordinator of Instructor and Course Evaluation System, Measurement and Research Division, 307 Engineering Hall, 1308 West Green, University of Illinois, Urbana, Ill. 61801.

Exhibit 9. Faculty Self-Evaluation.

For purposes of promotion, tenure, contract renewal, and increments

Name: _____

Date:_____ Appraisal for period from _____ to _____

Please answer the following questions. For questions involving rating scales, rate yourself 1 to 5 or NA for Not Applicable.

$$1 = \text{Never}$$
$$2 = \text{Seldom}$$
$$3 = \text{Average}$$
$$4 = \text{Usually}$$
$$5 = \text{Always}$$

1. The following are skills used in classroom instruction:

   A. I am well organized and present material
      clearly.   NA — 1 — 2 — 3 — 4 — 5
   B. I am readily available for consultation
      with students.   NA — 1 — 2 — 3 — 4 — 5
   C. I speak clearly, use illustrations to clarify
      the material, and summarize major
      points well.   NA — 1 — 2 — 3 — 4 — 5
   D. I encourage an open atmosphere where
      students feel free to ask questions and
      seek help if needed.   NA — 1 — 2 — 3 — 4 — 5
   E. I give examinations that reflect the
      important aspect of the courses taught.   NA — 1 — 2 — 3 — 4 — 5
   F. I am objective and able to substantiate
      grades given.   NA — 1 — 2 — 3 — 4 — 5
   G. I use a variety of teaching methods.   NA — 1 — 2 — 3 — 4 — 5

   H. What have you done differently from last year to improve your
      instructional capability and/or student learning? Were the
      changes successful? Why or why not?

   _____
   _____
   _____

2. In intellectual breadth and professional activities, I:

   *Related to Academic Discipline and Departmental or
   Divisional Responsibilities*

   A. Am well read beyond the subject I teach.   NA — 1 — 2 — 3 — 4 — 5
   B. Can suggest reading in any area of my
      general field.   NA — 1 — 2 — 3 — 4 — 5

continued on following page

Exhibit 9. Faculty Self-Evaluation *(continued).*

C. Make a positive contribution to the
    progress of my academic unit through
    committee participation.   NA − 1 − 2 − 3 − 4 − 5

D. What have you done to maintain and/or improve competence in
    your academic discipline?

    _____

    _____

    _____

*Related to College Duties and Professional Responsibilities
Outside the Classroom*

E. Discharge my college duties in an
    effective manner outside of the classroom.   NA − 1 − 2 − 3 − 4 − 5
F. Meet deadlines.   NA − 1 − 2 − 3 − 4 − 5
G. Cooperate with others.   NA − 1 − 2 − 3 − 4 − 5
H. Work well as a member of a committee.   NA − 1 − 2 − 3 − 4 − 5
I. Follow through on committee work by
    appropriate actions and communications.   NA − 1 − 2 − 3 − 4 − 5

J. Professional activities: List organizations in which you hold
    membership and any leadership roles.

    _____

    _____

    _____

K. List faculty committees, councils, ad hoc committees, etc.

    _____

    _____

    _____

3. In community service and/or consulting activities I:

    A. Make my talent and time available to the
        external community.   NA − 1 − 2 − 3 − 4 − 5
    B. Am asked to serve as a consultant to
        other organizations.   NA − 1 − 2 − 3 − 4 − 5

    Describe your participation in community and/or
    consulting activities.

    _____

    _____

    _____

4. In research activities, recognition, and personal development activities I:

    A. Have done research work in my field.   NA − 1 − 2 − 3 − 4 − 5
    B. Do original and creative work in artistic
        performances.   NA − 1 − 2 − 3 − 4 − 5

continued on following page

Exhibit 9. Faculty Self-Evaluation *(continued)*.

C. Express an interest in the research of
    my colleagues.   NA $-1-2-3-4-5$
D. Keep current with developments in
    my field.   NA $-1-2-3-4-5$
E. Do quality work.   NA $-1-2-3-4-5$

F. List conferences and/or workshops you attended during the
    past year.

_____

_____

_____

G. List awards and recognitions received during the past year.

_____

_____

_____

H. List what you have done in research, writing, artistic
    performances, etc.

_____

_____

_____

I. Responsibilities for development of proposals or special
    assignments for the department. Describe.

_____

_____

_____

Exhibit 10. Peer/Self-Appraisal of Faculty Service.

Faculty member _____

Dept. _____ Date _____

Appraiser _____ Title _____

The following elements reflect basic components of faculty service and relations.

Please rate the faculty member named above by drawing a circle around the number that most closely expresses your view.

		Low				High	Don't Know
1.	Attends committee and faculty meetings regularly.	1	2	3	4	5	X
2.	Does an appropriate share of institutional service assignments.	1	2	3	4	5	X
3.	Accepts service assignments willingly.	1	2	3	4	5	X
4.	Makes a positive contribution to assigned committees.	1	2	3	4	5	X
5.	Serves effectively as a committee chairperson.	1	2	3	4	5	X
6.	Maintains a professional and cooperative attitude in dealing with colleagues.	1	2	3	4	5	X
7.	Actively supports departmental and institutional goals.	1	2	3	4	5	X
8.	Is prompt and accurate with reports, grades, and so on.	1	2	3	4	5	X
9.	Is genuinely interested in assisting colleagues.	1	2	3	4	5	X
10.	Composite rating.	1	2	3	4	5	X

Nature of faculty assignments and services:

_____

_____

_____

You are invited to comment further on the effectiveness of this faculty member, especially in areas not covered by the questions.

_____

_____

Source: Seldin, 1980. Reproduced by permission.

Exhibit 11. Peer Appraisal of Research/Publication Work.

Faculty member _____

Dept. _____ Date _____

Appraiser _____ Title _____

Please indicate your appraisal of the faculty member named above in regard to the following factors by drawing a circle around the number that most closely expresses your view.

		Low				High	Don't Know
1.	How do you rate the adequacy of the research design (if applicable)?	1	2	3	4	5	X
2.	How do colleagues outside the department rate the importance of the research study/publication?	1	2	3	4	5	X
3.	Is the research study/publication closely related to the faculty member's area of teaching responsibility?	1	2	3	4	5	X
4.	How do you rate the quality of this publication?	1	2	3	4	5	X
5.	Were appropriate professional time and effort spent on this research study/publication?	1	2	3	4	5	X
6.	Compared to others in the department, how do you rate the research/publication performance of this faculty member?	1	2	3	4	5	X

7. What is this faculty member's greatest strength with regard to research/ publication? (Please elaborate.)

_____

_____

_____

8. What are his or her most serious shortcomings? (Please elaborate.)

_____

_____

_____

Source: Seldin, 1980. Reproduced by permission.

Exhibit 12. Peer Evaluation of Research Activity.

Faculty member _____

Dept. _____ Date _____

Evaluator _____

I typically have contact with this faculty member:

        _____ Daily   _____ Monthly

        _____ Weekly   _____ Infrequently

Listed below are statements that describe aspects of faculty research activity. For the faculty member named above, please circle the number that indicates the degree to which you feel each statement describes him or her.

Research Activity	Not Descriptive		Highly Descriptive			Doesn't Apply or Don't Know
1. Has gained national or international recognition.	1	2	3	4	5	X
2. Publishes articles in quality journals.	1	2	3	4	5	X
3. Publishes scholarly reviews of articles and books.	1	2	3	4	5	X
4. Gives papers at important conferences.	1	2	3	4	5	X
5. Is highly regarded by others in the same general field.	1	2	3	4	5	X
6. Is increasing research and publication activities.	1	2	3	4	5	X
7. Keeps current with developments in his or her field.	1	2	3	4	5	X
8. Attracts research funds and graduate students.	1	2	3	4	5	X

9. Compared to others in the department/division, how do you rate the overall research activity of this faculty member? (Please elaborate.)

_____

_____

_____

Appendix:
The Survey Instrument

The two-part form presented here is the survey instrument returned by the 616 liberal arts colleges participating in the nationwide study discussed in Chapter Three. It is reprinted so that readers may examine it first-hand.

Part I

EVALUATION OF OVERALL FACULTY PERFORMANCE

Instructions:

What factors are principally considered in evaluating a faculty member for promotion in rank, salary increase, or tenure? Please indicate the importance of each factor by placing a circle around one response in each row.

IBM Code ► Factors	(1) Major Factor	(2) Minor Factor	(3) Not A Factor	(4) Not Applicable
1. Classroom teaching	1	2	3	4
2. Supervision of graduate study	1	2	3	4
3. Supervision of honors program	1	2	3	4
4. Research	1	2	3	4
5. Publication	1	2	3	4
6. Public service	1	2	3	4
7. Consultation (government, business)	1	2	3	4
8. Activity in professional societies	1	2	3	4
9. Student advising	1	2	3	4
10. Campus committee work	1	2	3	4
11. Length of service in rank	1	2	3	4
12. Competing job offers	1	2	3	4
13. Personal attributes	1	2	3	4
14. Other (specify)	1	2	3	4

EVALUATION OF TEACHING PERFORMANCE

Instructions:

Please indicate the frequency with which each of the following types of information is used in your college in evaluating a faculty member's <u>teaching performance</u>. (Please circle <u>one</u> answer in each row.)

Types of information	(1) Always Used	(2) Usually Used	(3) Seldom Used	(4) Never Used
15. Systematic student ratings	1	2	3	4
16. Informal student opinions	1	2	3	4
17. Classroom visits	1	2	3	4
18. Colleagues' opinions	1	2	3	4
19. Scholarly research and publication	1	2	3	4
20. Student examination performance	1	2	3	4
21. Chair evaluation	1	2	3	4
22. Dean evaluation	1	2	3	4
23. Course syllabi and examinations	1	2	3	4
24. Long-term follow-up of students	1	2	3	4
25. Enrollment in elective courses	1	2	3	4
26. Alumni opinions	1	2	3	4
27. Committee evaluation	1	2	3	4
28. Grade distributions	1	2	3	4
29. Self-evaluation or report	1	2	3	4
30. Other (specify)	1	2	3	4

31. Do you routinely employ any special rating forms or other instruments in collecting data on teaching competence?
    Please circle the appropriate number.   Yes ___ 1 ___   No ___ 2 ___
    (If yes, please attach copies of these instruments.)

32. Has your institution developed research concerning the validity or usefulness of these instruments?
    Please circle the appropriate number.   Yes ___ 1 ___   No ___ 2 ___

Part II

EVALUATION OF SCHOLARSHIP/RESEARCH PERFORMANCE

Instructions:

Please indicate the frequency with which each of the following types of information is used in your college in evaluating a faculty member's scholarship/research performance. (Please circle one answer in each row.)

Types of information	(1) Always Used	(2) Usually Used	(3) Seldom Used	(4) Never Used
33. Publication in all professional journals	1	2	3	4
34. Articles in quality journals	1	2	3	4
35. Unpublished papers or reports	1	2	3	4
36. Papers at professional meetings	1	2	3	4
37. Citations in published materials	1	2	3	4
38. Books as sole or senior author	1	2	3	4
39. Books as junior author or editor	1	2	3	4
40. Monographs or chapters in books	1	2	3	4

Quality of research and publication as judged by:	(1) Always Used	(2) Usually Used	(3) Seldom Used	(4) Never Used
41. Peers at the institution	1	2	3	4
42. Peers at other institutions	1	2	3	4
43. Department chair	1	2	3	4
44. Academic dean	1	2	3	4
45. Self-evaluation	1	2	3	4
46. Grants or funding received	1	2	3	4
47. Referee or editor of professional journal	1	2	3	4
48. Honors or awards from profession	1	2	3	4
49. Other (specify)	1	2	3	4

Part III

EVALUATION OF COLLEGE SERVICE PERFORMANCE

Instructions:

Please indicate the frequency with which each of the following factors is used in your college in evaluating a faculty member's college service performance. (Please circle one answer in each row.)

Factors	(1) Major Factor	(2) Minor Factor	(3) Not A Factor	(4) Not Applicable
50. Service on department committee	1	2	3	4
51. Service on collegewide committee	1	2	3	4
52. Academic advising	1	2	3	4
53. Nonacademic student counseling	1	2	3	4
54. Willingness to teach undesirable courses	1	2	3	4
55. Adviser to student organizations	1	2	3	4
56. Service as student recruiter	1	2	3	4
57. Departmental administrative duties	1	2	3	4
58. Participation in campus symposia	1	2	3	4
59. Other (specify)	1	2	3	4

College Data: (Please circle the appropriate number for your college.)
60. Institutional control: Private 1   Public 2

YOUR COMMENTS ARE INVITED.   PLEASE USE REVERSE SIDE OF PAGE.

References

Acheson, K. A., and Gall, M. *Techniques in the Clinical Supervision of Teachers.* New York: Longman, 1980.

American Association of University Professors. *Policy Documents and Reports.* Washington, D. C.: American Association of University Professors, 1977.

American Association of University Professors. "A Preliminary Statement on Judicially Compelled Disclosure in the Nonrenewal of Faculty Appointments." Statement adopted by the Council of the American Association of University Professors, Washington, D.C., Nov. 21, 1980.

Aubrecht, J. D. "Teacher Effectiveness: Self-Determined Change." *American Journal of Physics,* 1978, *46* (4), 324–328.

Aubrecht, J. D., and Kramer, J. L. "Continuing Education Personnel Evaluation: Complexities, Perplexities, and Occasional Illuminations." *Continuum,* 1982, *46* (4), 41–48.

Balch, P. M. *Faculty Evalution in Higher Education: A Review of Court Cases and Implications for the 1980s.* Washington, D.C.: Educational Resources Information Center, U.S. Department of Education, 1980.

Berquist, W. H., and Phillips, S. R. *A Handbook for Faculty Development.* Washington, D.C.: Council for the Advancement of Small Colleges, 1975.

Bickel, R. D., and Brechner, J. A. (Eds.). *The College Administration and the Courts.* Asheville, N.C.: College Administration Publications, 1978.

Boyer, E. "Higher Education Should Do More than Imitate Its Corporate Rivals." *Chronicle of Higher Education,* May 25, 1983, p. 32.

Braskamp, L. A. "What Function Can Colleagues Have in the Evaluation of Instruction?" *NACTA Journal,* 1980, *24* (2), 16–21.

Braskamp, L. A., and Brown, R. D. *Utilization of Evaluation Information.* San Francisco: Jossey-Bass, 1980.

Braskamp, L. A., and others. *Guidebook for Evaluating Teaching.* Urbana: Measurement and Research Division, Office of Instructional Resources, University of Illinois, 1983.

Breneman, D. W. "The Coming Enrollment Crises: Focusing on the Figures." *Change Magazine,* 1983, *15* (2), 14–19.

"Calls for Computer Classes Swamping Colleges." *New York Times,* June 6, 1983, p. 1.

Centra, J. A. "Colleagues as Raters of Classroom Instruction." *Journal of Higher Education,* 1975, *46,* 327–337.

Centra, J. A. *Determining Faculty Effectiveness: Assessing Teaching, Research, and Service for Personnel Decisions and Improvement.* San Francisco: Jossey-Bass, 1979.

Centra, J. A. *Research Productivity and Teaching Effectiveness.* Princeton, N.J.: Educational Testing Service, 1981.

Chira, S. "Colleges Seeking New Approaches to Financial Aid." *New York Times,* Nov. 13, 1982, p. 25.

Cleary, T. *Getting Ready: A Checklist of Questions for the Teacher.* The Learning and Teaching Center, University of Victoria, British Columbia, n.d.

Cohen, P. A. "Student Ratings of Instruction and Student Achievement: A Meta-Analysis of Multisection Validity Studies." *Review of Educational Research,* 1981, *51,* 281–309.

Cohen, P. A., and McKeachie, W. J. "The Role of Colleagues in the Evaluation of College Teaching." *Improving College and University Teaching,* 1980, *28* (4), 147–154.

Cole, S., Cole, J. R., and Simon, G. A. "Chance and Consensus in Peer Review." *Science,* 1981, *214,* 881–886.

"College Provides Housing for Elderly." *New York Times,* May 5, 1983, sec. C, p. 11.

"Court Conditionally Orders College to Award Tenure." *Chronicle of Higher Education,* March 3, 1980, p. 9.

"Court Refuses to Review Texas Sex Bias Ruling," *Chronicle of Higher Education,* March 2, 1983, p. 12.

Cranton, P. A., and Geis, G. L. *Evaluating Teaching.* Montreal: Centre for Teaching and Learning Services, McGill University, 1982.

Dawson, J. A., and Caulley, D. M. "The Group Interview as an Evaluation Technique in Higher Education." *Educational Evaluation and Policy Analysis,* 1981, *3,* 61–66.

Denison, D. C. "Selling College in a Buyer's Market." *New York Times Magazine,* Apr. 10, 1983, p. 45.

Desruisseaux, P. "Federal Judge Upholds Women's Claim of Salary Discrimination at CUNY." *Chronicle of Higher Education,* Mar. 30, 1983, p. 30.

Dressel, P. L. *Handbook of Academic Evaluation.* San Francisco: Jossey-Bass, 1976.

Dubin, B., and Taveggia, T. C. *The Teaching-Learning Paradox: A Comparative Analysis of College Teaching Methods.* Eugene: Center for the Advanced Study of Educational Administration, University of Oregon, 1968.

Eble, K. E. *Professors as Teachers.* San Francisco: Jossey-Bass, 1972.

Eble, K. E. *The Craft of Teaching.* San Francisco: Jossey-Bass, 1976.

Eble, K. E. "Can Faculty Objectively Evaluate Teaching?" In G. French-Lazovik (Ed.), *Practices that Improve Teaching Evaluation.* San Francisco: Jossey-Bass, 1982.

Edwards, H., and Nordin, V. *Education and the Law.* Cambridge, Mass.: Institute for Educational Management, Harvard University, 1979.

Fields, C. M. "Council Probes Variations in Salaries of Male and Female Teachers." *Chronicle of Higher Education,* Dec. 2, 1981, p. 9.

Fields, C. M. "High Court Rejects Case of Professor Jailed for Not Revealing Tenure Vote." *Chronicle of Higher Education,* June 16, 1982, p. 1.

Fields, C. M. "How Does Equal Pay Act Apply to Colleges? Case in Oregon Raises the Issue." *Chronicle of Higher Education,* Feb. 23, 1983, p. 14.

Fiske, E. B. "Jailing of a Professor Heightens Fears for Campus Independence." *New York Times,* Sept. 14, 1980, p. 1.

Fiske, E. B. "The Courts in Tenure Cases: Must Faculty Disclose Votes?" *New York Times,* Dec. 1, 1981, sec. C, p. 1.

Fiske, E. B. "Money Is Key Issue at College Parley." *New York Times,* Oct. 17, 1982, p. 31.

Fiske, E. B. "Higher Education's New Economics." *New York Times Magazine,* May 1, 1983, p. 46.

"Former Professor at Tufts Wins $350,000 in Suit." *Chronicle of Higher Education,* June 1, 1983, p. 3.

French-Lazovik, G. *Evaluation of College Teaching.* Washington, D.C.: Association of American Colleges, 1976.

French-Lazovik, G. "Peer Review." In J. Millman (Ed.), *Handbook of Teacher Evaluation.* Beverly Hills: Sage, 1981.

"Growing Row over Peer Review." *Time,* Oct. 6, 1980, pp. 78–79.

Guzzetta, D. J. "Education's Quiet Revolution—Changes and Challenges." *Change Magazine,* 1982, *14* (6), 10–60.

Helling, B. *Looking for Good Teaching: A Guide to Peer Observation.* Northfield, Minn.: St. Olaf College, 1976.

Hildebrand, M., Wilson, R. C., and Dienst, E. R. *Evaluating University Teaching.* Berkeley: Center for Research and Development in Higher Education, University of California, 1971.

Hollander, P. *Legal Handbook for Educators.* Boulder, Colo.: Westview Press, 1978.

Holley, W. H., and Feild, H. S. "The Law and Performance Evaluation in Education: A Review of Court Cases and Implications for Use." *Journal of Law and Education,* 1977, *6* (4), 427–448.

Hoyt, D. P. *Background on the Uses and Misuses of Peer Evaluation: Perspectives from Another Campus.* Iowa City, Iowa: Unpublished manuscript, 1977.

Hyman, R. *Teaching: Vantage Points for Study.* Philadelphia: Lippincott, 1968.

"In Brief." *Chronicle of Higher Education,* April 6, 1983, p. 2.

Irby, D. M. "Evaluating Clinical Teaching in Medicine." *Journal of Medical Education,* 1981, *56,* 181–186.

Jackson, T. "Female Professors Gain Little Ground." *New York Times Education Supplement,* Jan. 9, 1983, p. 17.

Kaplin, W. A. *The Law of Higher Education: Legal Implications of Administrative Decision Making.* San Francisco: Jossey-Bass, 1978.

Kaplin, W. A. *The Law of Higher Education 1980.* San Francisco: Jossey-Bass, 1980.

Koffman, M. *An Interactive Computer-Based Evaluation System: Implications for Faculty Development.* Boston: Office of Instructional Development, Northeastern University, 1982.

Kronk, A. H., and Shipka, T. A. *Evaluation of Faculty in Higher Education.* Washington, D.C.: National Education Association, 1980.

Kulik, J. A., and McKeachie, W. J. "The Evaluation of Teachers in Higher Education." In F. N. Kerlinger (Ed.), *Review of Research in Education.* Itasca, Ill.: Peacock, 1975.

Latham, G. P., and Wexley, K. N. *Increasing Productivity Through Performance Appraisal.* Reading, Mass.: Addison-Wesley, 1981.

Leshner, A. I. "Innovation May Be the Answer to the Formidable Challenges of the 1980s and Beyond." *Chronicle of Higher Education,* Oct. 13, 1982, p. 64.

Lester, R. A. *Anti-Bias Regulations of Universities: Faculty Problems and Their Solutions.* New York: McGraw-Hill, 1979.

Levenstein, A. "Confidentiality and Due Process." *Newsletter* [of the National Center for the Study of Collective Bargaining in Higher Education and the Professions], 1981, *9* (4), 1–3.

Levinson-Rose, J., and Menges, R. J. "Improving College Teaching: A Critical Review of Research." *Review of Educational Research,* 1981, *51,* 403–434.

Lindsey, R. "University of California Hurt by Budget Cuts." *New York Times,* June 22, 1983, p. 1.

McCarthy, J., and Ladimer, I. *Resolving Faculty Disputes.* New York: American Arbitration Association, 1981.

McConnell, T. R., and Mortimer, K. D. *The Faculty in University Governance.* Berkeley: Center for Research and Development in Higher Education, University of California, 1971.

McFadden, R. D. "U.S. Court Rules Against City U. in Sex-Bias Suit." *New York Times,* Mar. 19, 1983, p. 1.

McIntyre, C. "Evaluation of College Teachers." *Criteria* [published by the University of Michigan Center for Research on Learning and Teaching], May 1977, pp. 1–6.

McKeachie, W. J. "Research in Teaching: The Gap Between Theory and Practice." In C. B. T. Lee (Ed.), *Improving College Teaching.* Washington, D.C.: American Council on Education, 1967.

McKeachie, W. J. "Student Ratings of Faculty: A Reprise." *Academe,* 1979, *65,* 384–397.

McKeachie, W. J. Personal communication, July 16, 1981.

Macnow, G. "Michigan to Study State Campuses: Some Could Shut." *Chronicle of Higher Education,* May 18, 1983, p. 1.

Maeroff, G. I. "City University Teacher Wins Right to Check on Tenure Denial." *New York Times,* Nov. 18, 1982a, sec. B, p. 3.

Maeroff, G. I. "Faculty Life Is Changed by Plight of the Colleges." *New York Times,* Mar. 8, 1982b, p. 15.

Maeroff, G. I. "Merit Pay for Teachers Versus Single Salary Schedule." *New York Times,* June 17, 1983, p. 17.

Magarrell, J. "Great Pessimism Voiced by Chiefs of Public Institutions." *Chronicle of Higher Education,* Dec. 15, 1982a, p. 8.

Magarrell, J. "Recession Hits State Support for Colleges." *Chronicle of Higher Education,* Oct. 20, 1982b, p. 1.

Magarrell, J. "Colleges' Energy Costs May Double if U.S. Lifts Limits on Gas Prices." *Chronicle of Higher Education,* Apr., 27, 1983a, p. 1.

Magarrell, J. "Eight Major Projects that Universities Have Developed." *Chronicle of Higher Education,* Apr. 20, 1983b, p. 9.

Magarrell, J. "Growth in State Funds for Colleges Expected to Slow Further in 1984." *Chronicle of Higher Education,* June 1, 1983c, p. 1.

Magarrell, J. "Many Universities Moving into Real-Estate Development Business as Need for Campus Expansion Eases." *Chronicle of Higher Education,* Apr. 20, 1983d, p. 8.

Magarrell, J. "Public-Private Competition Intensifying." *Chronicle of Higher Education,* May 25, 1983e, p. 1.

Marsh, H. W. "The Influence of Student, Course, and Instructor Characteristics in the Evaluation of University Teaching." *American Educational Research Journal,* 1980, *17,* 291–337.

"Math Professor in Texas Wins Discrimination Suit." *Chronicle of Higher Education,* March 2, 1983, p. 2.

Matthews, W. R., Jr. "College Students' Market." *New York Times,* May 30, 1983, p. 19.

Mattingly, E. "Publicity over Jailed Professor Obscures Problems at U. of Georgia." *Chronicle of Higher Education,* Sept. 29, 1980, p. 24.

Menges, R. J. "The New Reporters: Students Rate Instruction." In C. R. Pace (Ed.), *New Directions in Evaluating Learning and Teaching,* no. 4. San Francisco: Jossey-Bass, 1973.

Middleton, L. "Appeals Filed in Two Conflicting Tenure-Vote Cases." *Chronicle of Higher Education,* Dec. 9, 1981, p. 10.

Middleton, L. "Appeals Court Rejects 'Academic Freedom' as Professor's Defense in Tenure-Vote Case." *Chronicle of Higher Education,* Nov. 25, 1983, p. 1.

Miller, R. I. *The Assessment of College Performance.* San Francisco: Jossey-Bass, 1979.

Millman, J. *Handbook of Teacher Evaluation.* Beverly Hills: Sage, 1981.

Mitzman, B. "U. of Washington Plans to Drop Twenty-Four Degree Programs." *Chronicle of Higher Education,* Nov. 10, 1982a, p. 3.

Mitzman, B. "On Oregon's Campuses, the Refrain Is 'We Can't Cut Anything More.'" *Chronicle of Higher Education,* Dec. 1, 1982b, p. 6.

"Money-Shy Colleges Go Moonlighting." *U.S. News and World Report,* Nov. 26, 1979, p. 73.

National Research Council. *Career Outcomes in a Matched Sample of Men and Women Ph.D.s.* Washington, D.C.: National Research Council, 1981.

Nielsen, R. M., and Polishook, I. H. "The Vulnerable Academy." *Chronicle of Higher Education,* Jan. 19, 1981, p. 9.

O'Connell, W. R., and Wergin, J. F. "The Role of Administrators in Changing Teaching Evaluation Procedures." In G. French-Lazovik (Ed.), *New Directions for Teaching and Learning: Practices that Improve Teaching Evaluation.* San Francisco: Jossey-Bass, 1982.

O'Hanlon, J., and Mortensen, L. "Making Teacher Evaluation Work." *Journal of Higher Education,* 1980, *51,* 664–672.

Ory, J. C. "Item Placement and Wording Effects on Overall Ratings." *Educational Psychological Measurement,* 1982, *42,* 767–775.

Ory, J. C., and Braskamp, L. A. "Faculty Perceptions of the Quality and Usefulness of Three Types of Evaluative Information." *Research in Higher Education,* 1981, *15,* 271–282.

Outcalt, D., and others. *Task Force on the Evaluation of Teaching.* Berkeley: University of California, 1980.

Overall, J. U., and Marsh, H. W. "Students' Evaluations of Instruction: A Longitudinal Study of Their Stability." *Journal of Educational Psychology,* 1980, *72,* 321–325.

Overall, J. U., and Marsh, H. W. "Students' Evaluations of Teaching: An Update." *Research Currents/American Association for Higher Education Bulletin,* December 1982, pp. 9–12.

Perry, S. "Tenure Panelists Told They Must Disclose Votes." *Chronicle of Higher Education,* Nov. 24, 1982, p. 1.

"Personnel and Budget Procedures." *Minutes of Proceedings, Board of Higher Education, City of New York,* Dec. 18, 1967, pp. 598–602.

Peterson, P. L., and Walberg, H. J. (Eds.). *Research on Teaching: Concepts, Findings, and Implications.* Berkeley: McCutchan, 1980.

Polishook, I. H. "Peer Judgment and Due Process." In *Collective Bargaining and the Future of Higher Education: Proceedings of the Fifth Annual Conference, National Center for the Study of Collective Bargaining in Higher Education.* New York: National Center for the Study of Collective Bargaining in Higher Education, Baruch College, City University of New York, 1977.·

Polishook, I. H. "Academic Evaluation and Due Process." In G. French-Lazovik (Ed.), *Practices that Improve Teaching Evaluation.* San Francisco: Jossey-Bass, 1982.

"Professor Asks Supreme Court to Review Appellate Ruling on Tenure Vote." *Chronicle of Higher Education,* April 14, 1982, p. 15.

"Rights in Conflict: The Secrecy of the Tenure Vote." *Newsletter* [of the National Center for the Study of Collective Bargaining in Higher Education and the Professions], 1981, *9* (5), 1–4.

Ripply, R. M. *The Evaluation of Teaching in Medical Schools.* New York: Springer, 1981.

Ruckle, S. "Recession in Northwest Continues Squeeze on Higher Education — Are We Next?" *California Higher Education, 1* (8), 13–20.

Schumer, F. R. "A Question of Sex Bias at Harvard." *New York Times Magazine,* Oct. 18, 1981, pp. 96–104.

Scriven, M. "Value vs. Merit." *Evaluation News,* 1978, *8,* 1–3.

Scriven, M. "Summative Teacher Evaluation." In J. Millman (Ed.), *Handbook of Teacher Evaluation.* Beverly Hills, Calif.: Sage, 1981.

Scully, M. "Colleges, States Weigh Rules to Make Tenure Harder to Get, Easier to Lose." *Chronicle of Higher Education,* Dec. 8, 1982, p. 1.

Scully, M. "Colleges Seek Ways to 'Broaden the Revenue Base.'" *Chronicle of Higher Education,* Mar. 2, 1983, p. 5.

Seldin, P. *How Colleges Evaluate Professors.* New York: Blythe-Pennington, 1975a.

Seldin, P. "Students Now Get to Help Decide the Worth of Their Professors." *New York Times,* June 8, 1975b, "Week in Review," p. 8.

Seldin, P. *Teaching Professors to Teach.* New York: Blythe-Pennington, 1977.

Seldin, P. *Successful Faculty Evaluation Programs.* New York: Coventry, 1980.

Seldin, P. "Improving Faculty Evaluation Programs." Paper presented at the International Conference on Improving University Teaching. Tsukuba, Japan, 1981.

Seldin, P. "Improving Faculty Evaluation Systems." *Peabody Journal of Education,* 1982a, *59* (2), 93–99.

Seldin, P. "Self-Assessment of College Teaching." *Improving College and University Teaching,* No. 1, 1982b, *30* (2), 70–74.

Shanker, A. "Prof's Jailing Threatens College Quality." *New York Times,* Oct. 5, 1980, sec. E, p. 7.

Shingles, R. D. "Faculty Ratings: Procedures for Interpreting Student Evaluations." *American Educational Research Journal,* 1977, *14,* 459–470.

Shore, B. M., and others. *Guide to the Teaching Dossier: Its Preparation and Use.* Montreal: Centre for Teaching and Learning, McGill University, n.d.

Smock, H. R., and Crooks, T. J. "A Plan for the Comprehensive Evaluation of College Teaching." *Journal of Higher Education,* 1973, *44,* 577–586.

"Survey Finds Few Women on Business-School Faculties." *Chronicle of Higher Education,* June 15, 1983, p. 2.

"Text of Appeals-Court Opinions in Georgia Tenure-Vote Case." *Chronicle of Higher Education,* Nov. 25, 1981, p. 14.

"Theologian Denied Tenure Settles with Fordham." *Chronicle of Higher Education,* Jan. 26, 1983, p. 3.

"Thirty-seven Women Settle Case Against University of Minnesota." *Chronicle of Higher Education,* May 4, 1983, p. 2.

Tucker, A. *Chairing the Academic Department.* Washington, D.C.: American Council on Education, 1981.

Uniform Guidelines on Employee Selection Procedures. 43 *Federal Register* 38290.

"University of Oregon Rehires Woman Who Charged Bias." *Chronicle of Higher Education,* March 3, 1983, p. 2.

"University of District of Columbia Settles Race Bias Suit." *Chronicle of Higher Education,* May 11, 1983, p. 2.

Watkins, B. T. "Gifts to Colleges Rise by 15 Percent, to $4.86 Billion." *Chronicle of Higher Education,* Apr. 27, 1982, p. 7.

Watkins, B. T. "The Cost of Recruiting a Student Is on the Rise, Survey Finds." *Chronicle of Higher Education,* May 4, 1983a , p. 7.

Watkins, B. T. "Eight-Year Bias Dispute at Canisius Goes to Court." *Chronicle of Higher Education,* Jan. 19, 1983b, p. 10.

Watkins, B. T. "Higher Education Now Big Business for Big Business." *Chronicle of Higher Education,* Apr. 13, 1983c, p. 1.

Weisman, S. "Reagan Attacks U.S. School Aid in Jersey Speech." *New York Times,* May 22, 1983, p. 1.

Wharton, C. R., Jr. "Enrollment: Higher Education's Window of Vulnerability." *Change Magazine, 15* (2), 20–22.

Whitman, N., and Weiss, E. *Faculty Evaluation: The Use of Explicit Criteria for Promotion, Retention, and Tenure.* AAHE-ERIC Higher Education Research Report No. 2. Washington, D.C.: American Association for Higher Education, 1982.

Wilson, L. *The Academic Man.* New York: Oxford University Press, 1942.

Winkler, K. J. "When It Comes to Journals, Is More Really Better?" *Chronicle of Higher Education,* Apr. 14, 1982, p. 21.

Winkler, K. J. "Faculty Wary of Plan to Close Utah College, Change Its Name, and Reopen a Day Later." *Chronicle of Higher Education,* Feb. 23, 1983a, p. 11.

Winkler , K. J. "Feminist Professor versus Stanford: A Tenure Test Case." *Chronicle of Higher Education,* Feb. 16, 1983b, p. 5.

Winkler, K. J. "Idaho Warned It Could Lose 100-Year Investment in Colleges." *Chronicle of Higher Education,* Jan. 26, 1983c, p. 9.

Yarrow, A. "Gypsy Scholars Roam Academic Landscape." *New York Times,* Jan. 10, 1982, p. 15.

Index